FROM GRIM TO
GREEN PASTURES

OTHER BOOKS BY RICHARD L. MORGAN

Graceful Aging: Sermons for Third Agers

Is There Life after Divorce in the Church?

No Wrinkles on the Soul:
A Book of Readings for Older Adults

I Never Found That Rocking Chair:
God's Call at Retirement

FROM GRIM TO GREEN PASTURES

Meditations for the Sick and Their Caregivers

RICHARD L. MORGAN

Foreword by
ARTHUR W. FRANK

UPPER
ROOM BOOKS
NASHVILLE

FROM GRIM TO GREEN PASTURES:
Meditations for the Sick and Their Caregivers

©1994 Richard L. Morgan

ed.

.ll rights reserved.

are from *The Holy Bible,*
ght ©1973, 1978, 1984,
International Bible Society and used by permission of
Zondervan Bible Publishers.

Scripture quotations designated NJB are taken from *The New Jerusalem Bible,* published and copyright ©1985 by Darton, Longman & Todd, Ltd. and Doubleday, a division of Bantam, Doubleday, Dell Publishing Group, Inc., and are used by permission.

Scripture quotations designated NKJV are from *The New King James Version.* Copyright ©1979, 1980, 1982, Thomas Nelson, Inc., Publishers, and used by permission.

Scripture quotations marked NRSV are from The New Revised Standard Version. Copyright ©1989 by the Division of Christian Education of the National Council of Churches of Christ in the USA, and used by permission.

See page 190 for acknowledgments.

Cover Design: Jim Bateman
Cover Photograph: Ron Dahlquist\Superstock
ISBN 0-8358-0708-8
Library of Congress Catalog Card Number: 94-60662
Printed in the United States of America.

To my sisters, primary caregivers:
Patricia, who ministers to the frail elderly
and
Mary Ann, who nurses the sick.

And to my wife,
Alice Ann,
who is my primary caregiver.

CONTENTS

Foreword

FOR THE DAY WHEN I AM ILL AGAIN, I keep a mental list of books I would take to the hospital. *From Grim to Green Pastures* joins that list. As a witness to illness, Dick Morgan tells the truth: The pastures *are* grim. But this truth also contains a promise. Dick Morgan's fellowship of stories about illness creates a space for hope. He reminds us that the only way to grace is through grim pastures.

When I had a heart attack and then cancer, I was one of those patients who writes "no religious preference" on my hospital admissions forms. Part of my good luck with these illnesses was that I went in without any particular faith. Many people would not count this as luck, but I do. Too many people's faith causes them more problems than it brings comfort; at worst, their loss of faith compounds other losses. Since I had nothing to lose, I was free to discover a faith that came out of suffering.

People lose faith because their suffering blows away what they thought they were entitled to expect. One expectation is how they will be treated by those with whom they share their faith—friends, family, and clergy. As Dick Morgan knows, family can turn out to be more demanding than sympathetic. Friends act threatened by one of their circle becoming seriously ill; rather than being a comfort, they have to be reassured. Clergy can reduce illness experience to generic triviality. Too often in my hospital stays I overheard chaplains who were visiting my roommate begin with some general banter, ignore the specifics of the illness entirely, and end with a prayer that could have been for anyone, anywhere. Admirable sentiments were expressed, but what was missing was any personal *confrontation* with suffering. Did those clergy themselves doubt the power of their faith to confront the suffering the ill person faced?

The other expectation that can be blown away by serious illness is that faith somehow protects against suffering and loss. Too many people still treat faith as a deal with God: they do their part and God will do his. These people forget that some of the holiest people of this century have died of cancer. God *does* do his part, but assuring health is not included.

So as Dick Morgan's title truthfully says, the pastures are *grim*. Most books would avoid that word. They want to sugarcoat illness, so that healthy people can be protected from their fears. But the seriously ill cannot afford the pretense that illness is not part of life and does not involve real suffering. The ill are not frightened by the word *grim;* for them that word affirms the reality of their experience. The ill are ready to hear the message of the Prophets and the Psalmist that we need to recognize how bad things are in order to become open to the presence of God.

What I learned from critical illnesses is the necessity of finding spiritual meaning in suffering. Dick Morgan provides one of the best guidebooks to finding that meaning. Those who have ears, let them listen, the Gospel writers frequently admonish. Dick Morgan has ears; he hears beyond the clichés of what we are supposed to say about illness. He has the ear for just the right Bible reading to give meaning to experiences that ill persons undergo every day, with stories from his own illness providing a bridge. When ill people can recognize their own stories told in Bible passages, then the Bible becomes a living experience of faith. Pain is still pain, but it becomes part of a pattern of human life that we not only share but can glorify.

Finding Dick Morgan's sort of faith through illness is more than luck. Such a faith transforms what was called luck into what becomes known as grace. Whether you read this book as a pastoral guide through illness or as spiritual preparation for the day you too will become ill, it can bring grace to suffering: the grace of understanding your own luck, good and bad, as the working of the Spirit in your life. The grim pastures can become springs.

ARTHUR W. FRANK, author
At the Will of the Body:
Reflections on Illness

Preface

IT WAS EARLY OCTOBER, AND THE WORLD outside my sick room signaled the end of summer. Yet I felt winter had already descended upon me, as I struggled to overcome severe complications from surgery. Unlike other surgeries I had experienced, this one had been devastating; it left me weakened, shattered, and frightened to death. Weeks later, a nurse told me, "The doctor was really worried about you." Much of the ordeal remains a blur, obscured by medication and the grace of God.

During the long days and nights of convalescence, I found comfort in remembering passages of scripture hidden in my heart. At times I felt like the author of Psalm 41: "He will never get up from the place where he lies" (41:8*b*, NIV). I yearned for some book of devotions that would speak to me, but none seemed available.

Max Lerner has said, "The greatest threat anyone with a radical illness runs is the threat to the continuity of selfhood. If that gets shattered, there is nothing to fight back with." My active life had been put on hold, but I was still a writer. I decided to record my experience in a journal and later compose a book of spiritual readings for others who face illness. I suppose that being able to write while flat on my back was one sure way to reassure myself that the major currents of my life were still flowing. Although medical people had given me helpful directions on how to care for my wounds when I left the hospital, no one addressed my soul needs. I felt out of control, severely in need of spiritual support. Prescriptions scribbled on a doctor's pad and directions from a nurse's clipboard just don't meet every need.

I have no complaint, especially when I consider how much other brave people have suffered. I stand in awe at how they have handled pain. What they suffered might well have devastated me. But *any* sickness is difficult, especially if it touches you. Job's Adversary knew that well when he said, "But stretch out your hand and lay a finger on his bone and flesh; I warrant you, he will curse you to your face" (Job 2:5, NJB). When surgery is done on someone else, it may be minor; but any surgery performed on me is major!

Frederick Buechner has written,

> In everything that has happened to us over the years God was offering us possibilities of new life and healing which, though we may have missed them at the time, we can still choose and be brought to life by and healed by them all years later.

I assure you that I found little possibilities for new life at first. It was only months later that I began to perceive how God was present in my suffering and then began to unravel the mystery.

From Grim to Green Pastures is a book of meditations for those who face sickness. More than five hundred years before Christ, an ancient Greek writer observed, "There is no mortal whom sorrow and disease do not touch." If not now, someday you will walk into the grim pastures. However, beyond are the green pastures of God's love and care.

From Grim to Green Pastures is also a book for caregivers, helping you to understand that what happens *inside* a sick person is as significant as what is done *to* them. As you walk with us and hold our hands,

may your presence embody the words found on the
office walls of my physician,

> Give me eyes that see the source of ill,
> Hands with the touch that heals;
> Ears that hear the cry of pain,
> A voice that comforts,
> A heart that feels.
> —*Source Unknown*

At the door of a Christian hospital:

O God,
  make the door of this house wide enough
  to receive all who need human love and fellowship,
  and a heavenly Father's care;
  and narrow enough to shut out
  all envy, pride, and hate.

Make its threshold smooth enough
  to be no stumbling block to children,
  nor to straying feet,
  but rugged enough to turn back the tempter's power:
  make it a gateway to thine eternal life.
                    Bishop Thomas Ken

I

The Inner World of Sickness

Illness is the night-side of life, a more onerous citizenship.

Everyone who is born holds dual citizenship, in the kingdom

of the well and in the kingdom of the sick.

Although we prefer to use only the good passport,

sooner or later each of us is obliged, at least for a spell,

to identify ourselves as citizens of that other place.

SUSAN SONTAG

1

What Does It Mean to Be Sick?
READ MARK 5:24-34

He said to her, "Daughter, your faith has made you well. Go in peace and be healed of your disease."
(Mark 5:34, NRSV)

THE WOMAN IN THE CROWD HAD BEEN SICK for twelve years with an uncontrollable hemorrhage. Despite endless visits to doctors, she had grown worse instead of better. Her sickness had rendered her ceremonially unclean, a social outcast, unfit for marriage or suitable for divorce. She was a nobody living with a problem for which there seemed to be no cure.

She had to break the Law to be healed, for by law she could not touch a holy man. From that wounded center of her life, knowing that all medical recourses had failed, she reached out in desperation and faith to touch Jesus. Her faith was so strong that she was healed before Jesus knew it. "Who touched me?" he asked. Even in that milling, jostling crowd, Jesus felt the touch of faith.

During the long weeks of recovering from serious complications from surgery, I identified with this nameless woman. My illness had left me drained of life and spiritually exhausted. My whole life had been undermined. Sickness is more than physical discomfort. It is dis-ease, jarring our whole person.

Arthur W. Frank has said, "Illness talk is a story about moving from a perfectly comfortable body to one that forces me to ask, "What's happening to *me*? Not *it*, but *me*." Medical technology often limits sickness to what happens to our bodies, instead of realizing how it affects our whole lives.

When Jesus asked, "Who touched me?" the woman crept forward, confessing that touch, for her actions could have made him unclean. For years no one had touched her, or anything she had touched. Now her touch of faith brought healing.

John Sanford says that "her illness was an essential step on her way to wholeness. . . . If she had been cured by well-intentioned doctors, she would have overcome her malady, but she would not have been changed and renovated in soul and spirit as well as in body." Driven by her desperate need, led by her faith, she found her way to the Great Physician who transformed her life and named her "Daughter."

Sickness affects our whole being. It means entering a strange world that only those who have been there can *begin* to understand. During my illness I learned the importance of the inner life of the spirit and realized that healing means more than feeling better. It is moving from dis-ease to wholeness.

GREAT PHYSICIAN,
We pray this prayer of faith,
The healing of His seamless dress
Is by our beds of pain;
We touch Him in life's throng and press,
And we are whole again.
—John Greenleaf Whittier

2

Living under Water
READ PSALM 42

Deep is calling to deep by the roar of your cataracts,
all your waves and breakers have rolled over me.
(Psalm 42:7, NJB)

SEFRA KOBRIN PITZELE HAS WRITTEN, "THE LOSS of normal good health can rock even the strongest person. In one fragile moment our life seems in shambles. . . . We wonder if we'll ever get through this suffering. For a while it seems as if *we are living under water*, nothing is clear or straightforward" (italics mine).

The psalmist felt that life had engulfed him. "All your waves and breakers have rolled over me." Living in the territory where the Jordan River had its origin, he heard the mighty thunderings of the mountain waterfalls and felt overwhelmed. It may well be that he was sick. We do not know. His whole life seemed overcome by some threat.

Facing surgery or sickness is like living under water. No one enters a hospital free from fears. There is always the fear that the doctor has made the wrong diagnosis or perhaps hasn't told you the whole story of your illness. Lurking behind the scenes stands the fear of death. You feel out of control, panicky, and fragmented.

Medical people try to help, but they often fail to realize what it feels like to be sick. They cannot begin to realize how we resent strangers who come at us with their vials and needles, often taking more blood than we think we have. What do they know (unless they have been patients) of the feeling of being victims, with privacy invaded and dignity denied?

And how can others understand our feelings when we are wheeled through white corridors to operating rooms with their blinking lights and unreal sounds?

Even after we return home, there remain long hours of restricted life, our normalcy disrupted. One writer, reflecting on his youthful travels in southern France, wrote, "I was free to wander, free to hope, and free to live." During sickness there is no such freedom; we are at the mercy of others.

There were moments in my convalescence, while I was confined for weeks to a few rooms, that I fantasized how it would be if I were always so restricted, an old man, homebound, unable to drive or care for myself. I felt overwhelmed, drowned by the thought.

The psalmist found hope in God's presence. "By day the Lord directs his love, at night his song is with me—a prayer to the God of my life" (Psalm 42:8, NIV). Dealing with illness, feeling overwhelmed by it, can cause us to reach out in faith to God. We call upon resources of faith to meet the challenge. God does come . . . even as the "waves and breakers" roll over us. When we feel drowned by our sickness, God comes and stands with us.

COMPASSIONATE LORD,
We confess we do despair when sickness
seems to overwhelm us.
You understand how we feel. Grant us your presence
when the waves roll over us, and calm our fears.
AMEN.

Every Sick Person Has a Story
READ MARK 1:39-45

Instead he went out and began to talk freely,
spreading the news.
(Mark 1:45a, NIV)

THE LEPER HAD BEEN TOLD BY JESUS TO KEEP QUIET about his healing. But he went out and began to tell everyone his story. He had reason to celebrate his recovery. People who experience sickness have a compulsive need to talk about it.

Martin L. Smith says, "Stories are the chief way human beings make sense of their experience. Even when life is hard and complex we can survive and maintain our sanity if our experiences can be told as a story with a thread holding the drama together."

Too many sick persons are deprived of conversation about their sickness. Arthur Kleinman distinguishes between *disease,* defined as physical symptoms or damage visible to a physician, and *illness,* the patient's subjective experience of the same illness. Doctors and nurses use "medicalese" to talk about our illnesses, but rarely do they allow the sick person to say how he or she feels.

The person who is sick feels compelled to come to terms with the experience and cannot help talking about it. The healing process cannot be bottled up or put on a shelf. But a taboo still exists in our society that you don't talk about your operation or sickness.

It helped me to talk about my feelings with my wife and close friends. Bernie Siegel, in *How to Live between Office Visits*, says it clearly:

> The story is the patient's metaphor. The metaphor can help you see inside an individual; it can help you gently cut through to what is actually significant for him or her. By entering in this way you enter into the sacred space of the individual you're trying to help. You're not just staying on the outside, writing prescriptions; rather, like a war buddy, you are entering into the heat of the battle and the sacredness of that individual's life.

Every time we experience sickness, we reminisce about former illnesses. Lying beneath the white sheets staring at the ceiling gives ample time to reflect. Part of our life story revolves around our experiences of sickness.

Into my mind came past sicknesses. I remembered being a child of six suffering with pneumonia in the days when there were no "magic bullets." I recalled recovering from second surgeries to correct some glaring mistakes made in the original surgeries. Endless struggles with health issues have plagued me throughout most of my life. Yes, we all have stories of our sickness . . . and health.

Let the day come when physicians, nurses, clergy, and family members say to the sick person, "Tell me how *you* feel about this sickness."

LOVING FATHER,
*You are always there when no one else wants to hear
us tell about our operation or sickness. Thanks for listening.*
AMEN.

A Kind of Madness
READ MARK 5:1-20

Where can I go from your Spirit?
Where can I flee from your presence?
If I go up to the heavens, you are there;
If I make my bed in the depths, you are there.
(Psalm 139:7-8, NIV)

I HAVE ALWAYS FELT COMPASSION FOR THE MAN called the "Gerasene Demoniac." His madness forced him to live in a cemetery, avoided by everyone and an enigma to himself. It may have been that someone he loved was buried in that lonely place, so he lived there, unable to free himself from the memory.

When he saw Jesus from a distance, he begged for mercy. Jesus kindly asked him, "What is your name?" No one had asked him that for years. Everyone was terrified to be close to him. Jesus walked with that man into the depths of his soul where no one had been, and healed his whole life. The people of the area were amazed to find this town clown "dressed and in his right mind."

Sickness is a form of madness, a strange experience where feelings are intensified and behavior exaggerated. Paul Tournier, the great physician of the soul, has said,

The sick person has also a new place to accept, to make his. This new, unknown place is the state of sickness. His place henceforth is his bed. . . . and then there is silence, the long silence that is difficult to fill when one is unused to it. . . . In the silence unaccustomed thoughts come into the sick person's mind, so that he wonders if they are not abnormal.

The demoniac had been avoided by everyone. People feared that his demons might invade them, so they kept their polite distance. To be sick is to be a stranger; most other people cannot relate to illness because of their own issues. As the ancient *Talmud* says, "We do not see things as *they* are; we see things as *we* are." We might add, "We do not see people as *they* are, but as *we* are." So, unless we are of the medical profession, clergy, or intimate family members, we tend to shy away from the sick. Very few people really try to understand, and we yearn for those who will call us by name and reach out to be with us in the depths of our experience.

The Gerasene's story had a happy ending. A sick man was made well by the compassion and love of Jesus. For him, madness was a journey of discovery from which he returned with insights about himself and his faith unknown to those who never embark on that voyage. As we work through our confusion and scattered lives, when everything seems out of focus and shattered, may we too find that healing touch of the One who knows our name and can bring order to our lives.

GOD OF MERCY,
Help us to recall how many times Jesus reached out to those who hurt,
especially when no one else seemed to care.
May we find that healing power right now.
AMEN.

Those Post-Op Blues
READ 1 KINGS 19:1-12

*Why are you cast down, O my soul,
and why are you disquieted within me? Hope in God.*
(Psalm 42:11, NRSV)

I COULDN'T UNDERSTAND WHY I WAS SO DEPRESSED. I had returned to the familiar surroundings of my home. The biopsy showed no cancer. It was understandable for me to be depressed in the hospital, especially since surgery had not gone as well as I had expected, and I had had some excruciating moments of pain. Now that was over, and yet my homecoming had not ended my depression.

Elijah was deeply depressed. He had not gone through surgery, but Queen Jezebel had surely cut him down. She had put out a contract on his life, so he fled across the desert and finally collapsed beneath a broom tree, exhausted and ready to die.

I wrote in my journal: "It has been several weeks since the surgery, and I see so little progress. I get so depressed wondering if I will be an invalid forever."

Norman Cousins saw a striking connection between reassurance and effective medical care for persons who experience sickness. He wrote,

Illness is a terrifying experience. Something is happening that people don't know how to deal with. They are reaching out not just for medical help but for ways of thinking about catastrophic illness. They are reaching out for hope.

Elijah must have remembered his great victory at Mount Carmel, only to become depressed when he wondered if that was the end of his ministry. It seemed a Pyrrhic victory now that Jezebel's henchmen were set on ending his life.

Now I know why I was so depressed at home. Surrounded by all the symbols of my work, I felt angry and frustrated at my sickness. Being at home actually intensified my depression, for the familiar surroundings brought into sharper focus my loss of mobility and usefulness. Even the smallest routines of my life—going downstairs, working in the yard, mowing the grass—had been disrupted.

Depression is a real part of the sickness experience. Arthur W. Frank says, "Too few people, whether medical staff, family, or friends, seem willing to accept the possibility that depression may be the ill person's most appropriate response to the situation."

Elijah took time to go into the wilderness until he heard the gentle whisper. There is hope in God, for him and for us.

LIGHT OF OUR DARKNESS,
When we let our sickness get us down,
help us to look up to you and beyond ourselves.
AMEN.

6

Enforced Spaces of Silence
READ LUKE 1:5-22

For God alone my soul waits in silence;
from him comes my salvation.
(Psalm 62:1, NRSV)

DURING ILLNESS THERE ARE BOUND TO BE enforced spaces of silence. Waiting for surgery and recovering while in the hospital always mean some empty spaces of silence. Even at home, except for some conversation with family or close friends, life slows down to a turtle pace, and silence becomes more than a word.

During those long hours at home, my mind often focused on Zechariah. When the angel told him that his aged wife Elizabeth would have a child, he wondered how such a thing could happen. I guess that he completely forgot Abraham and Sarah's old-age miracle. For this lack of faith, Zechariah had to be silent for nine months.

Enforced spaces of silence come to sick people. But these moments can become times of spiritual renewal. It is a sad commentary on our age that we are addicted to noise. Movement, activity, and hectic schedules are our watchwords. We are less and less comfortable with silence, and we resist it. Yet it can be a time of spiritual growth.

Consider the beauty of silence. We stare in silence at the miracle of birth and stand speechless at the grave of a loved one. In hospital waiting rooms we wait in silence in little groups, holding one another's hands. Silence is the language of the soul before the mysteries of life and the presence of God.

In my quiet times I was forced to dig deep into my soul and wait for God. I read the scriptures and spiritual books, and prayed in the silence. It was a time of spiritual rebirth.

Sue Monk Kidd, in her book *When the Heart Waits*, tells the old Carolina story of a country boy who had the great talent of carving beautiful dogs out of wood. Every day he would sit on the porch, whittling and letting the shavings fall where they might. One day, a visitor, greatly impressed, asked him the secret of his art. "I just take a block of wood and whittle off the parts that don't look like a dog," he replied.

So it is with soul-making when we work through sickness. We have to whittle away the parts that are not heart and soul of our true self.

The enforced time of silence became a kind of spiritual retreat for Zechariah before the birth of his son, John. So for us, when sickness slows us down and silence takes over, we can make these moments a time of spiritual growth. "For God alone my soul waits in silence."

SILENT MYSTERY,
Settle us, silence us, in this time of sickness.
"Drop thy still dews of quietness, till all our strivings cease;
Take from our souls the strain and stress, and let our ordered
lives confess the beauty of thy peace."
AMEN.

Like a Spinning Top
READ ROMANS 12:3-8

*For by the grace given me I say to every one of you:
Do not think of yourself more highly than you ought, but
rather think of yourself with sober judgement, in accordance
with the measure of faith God has given you.*
(Romans 12:3, NIV)

CHARLES LAMB, IN HIS SHORT ESSAY "The Convalescent," vividly describes how egocentric sick people can be:

> How sickness enlarges the dimensions of a man's self
> to himself! He is his own exclusive object. Supreme
> selfishness is inculcated upon him as his only duty....
> He has nothing to think of but how to get well.

How true! When a person gets sick, she resembles a spinning top, with everyone and everything revolving around her needs. Family members are expected to forget their needs and become preoccupied with the sick person. A former member of my church had back surgery, and when I visited him to offer my concern, he said, "Don't feel bad for me. I never had such attention in my life, and I enjoy every minute of it."

Being sick usually means we become the center of the universe. Everyone is expected to wait on us, not just with food and medicine but with undivided attention. They put their lives on hold while we get well.

It *is* important that sick people get extra love and care. Our lives are disrupted, and we need all the kindness we can get. But we can become too self-centered and forget the needs of others, especially those who care for us. I often wonder if anyone realizes what family members go through when they are caring for a sick person. We need to be more patient with those who care for us. Paul counseled the Philippian Christians,

> Do nothing out of selfish ambition or vain conceit, but in humility consider others better than yourselves. Each of you should look not only to your own interests, but also to the interests of others.
>
> (Philippians 2:3-4, NIV)

It is not easy to look beyond our own pain when sickness strikes us. For a while, all we can think about is *our* discomfort. But being so self-centered becomes boring and constraining.

Christ is our example, who in his hour of extreme pain looked down from the cross and remembered others: the dying thief, his grieving mother, and even those who were crucifying him. He was no spinning top in that hour, but a model of love. Reaching out in love and compassion to others was the touchstone of his whole life. "The Son of Man came not to be ministered unto, but to minister" (Mark 10:45a, KJV).

Let us who suffer remember our Lord and be sensitive and considerate of the needs of others.

SUFFERING LORD,
Help us not to be so preoccupied with our pain that we cannot recognize or help others who need us.
AMEN.

Be Patient with the Doctor
READ ECCLESIASTICUS 38:1-8

There are times when good health depends on doctors.
(Ecclesiasticus 38:13, NJB)

IT IS STRANGE TO FIND WORDS OF PRAISE for doctors in the scriptures. In the Old Testament doctors were not held in high esteem. God was the healer, and consultations with doctors were seen as an admission of failure and a lack of faith. Illness was viewed as punishment by God for one's sins, so healing included confession, penitence, and reconciliation with God. Not only was there little room for the physician among the ancient Hebrews, but they were often referred to in disparaging terms.

Even today, in the midst of medical marvels, too many of us still indulge in "doctor bashing." We cast doctors as the chief villains in the health care crisis. We protest their outrageous charges, complain about their lack of interest in us as persons, and always grumble about how long they make us wait in their offices.

Ben Sira, the writer of Ecclesiasticus, commends physicians and even says, "Treat the doctor with the honor that is his due, in consideration of his services.... Let the doctor take over—the Lord created him too—do not let him leave you, for you need him" (Ecclesiasticus 38:1,12, NJB).

Nothing is more important in the healing process than the relationship between physician and patient.

When there is open communication between them, a cooperative effort is unleashed which has a powerful effect on the healing process.

Paul Tournier comments, "How much better when, along with the technical skill [the doctor] has also those human qualities which make the doctor a healer of persons!" There are times when good health depends on doctors. We put our trust in the hands of surgeons when we enter that dark unknown. We need to listen to their counsel as they work for our wellness. And we need to be patient when they make mistakes, for they, too, are human.

Anatole Broyard, who wrote *Intoxicated by My Illness* before his death from prostate cancer, talks about the kind of doctor he wants to have, and to talk to, and to be with:

> Not every patient can be saved, but his illness may be eased by the way the doctor responds to him—and in responding to him the doctor may save himself. . . . It may be necessary to give up some of his authority in exchange for his humanity, but as the old family doctors knew, this is not a bad bargain. . . . He has little to lose and everything to gain by letting the sick man into his heart.

Isn't it significant that Paul, who suffered from some incurable "thorn in the flesh," called his doctor, Luke, the "beloved physician" (Col. 4:14)? We also owe debts of eternal gratitude to doctors whose hands of healing have preserved our lives, and saved those of our loved ones.

HEALER OF SOULS,
Give us patience with our doctors.
AMEN.

That Double Bind
READ GALATIANS 1:11-24

*To everything there is a season, A time for every purpose
under heaven . . . A time to embrace, And
a time to refrain from embracing.
(Ecclesiastes 3:1,5b, NKJV)*

SAUL OF TARSUS EXPERIENCED A SHATTERING moment of
truth and light on the road to Damascus. His whole life
was transformed. At first he needed time to be alone, so
he went to Arabia for three years. There he could think
through this life-changing event. He needed to be with
God before he could be with people.

People who experience surgery and/or sickness
face a double bind. *The sicker we are, the more private we
become.* We don't want our privacy invaded, nor do we
want to be totally forgotten. It is true in the hospital,
where we need our privacy and shudder at the thought
of a mob of people surrounding our sickbed. But a time
does come later on when we crave visits.

During my days in the hospital, and even in the
first weeks at home, I wanted to be left alone. I was glad
when one of my friends called and said, "I would come
to see you, but now I know you need to be left alone."
How thoughtful. It is difficult to show our wounds or
share our pain with everyone. We just want our closest
family to be present.

Later on, however, Paul craved the companionship
of the early Christians. So he went to Jerusalem to bond

with Peter and the other disciples. Already the prayers of Stephen and the kindness of Ananias had touched his life. And it was Barnabas who became his mediator to the others.

As I began to feel somewhat better, I wanted to hear from family and friends. Too often they forget you when you are discharged from the hospital. They assume that if you are well enough to go home, you are well on the road to recovery. They don't know about the lonely pit stops after you round the turn of recovery.

Rather than intruding into their busy schedules, you tend to withdraw and wait for the telephone that never seems to ring. All too often we give and receive mixed messages. We say, "I'm doing fine, and I need to be alone," but the tone of our voice means, "I am lonely. Please call me." They say, "I know you want some privacy for a while," but in reality they are saying, "We'd rather not face you now."

A double bind. A need for privacy and yet a hunger for attention. It is a wise person who can be open and honest and tell family and friends what their needs are. There are creative ways in which family and friends can honor privacy and yet provide care. A well-chosen card, a reassuring telephone call, and an offer to be there when needed are ways to provide for both times of the sickness journey.

HEALER OF PERSONS,
Tend thy sick ones, O Lord Christ; rest thy weary ones;
bless thy dying ones; soothe thy suffering ones;
shield thy joyous ones; and all for thy Love's sake.
(Prayer of St. Augustine)

Minding the Body / Mending the Mind
READ MARK 2:1-12

*Beloved, I pray that all may go well with you and that
you may be in good health, just as it is well with your soul.
(3 John 2, NRSV)*

SO MUCH OF JESUS' MINISTRY WAS SPENT IN HEALING that
if you took a copy of the Gospels and cut out all
mention of healing or of casting out demons, your
Gospels would be greatly reduced. The healing of the
paralytic man is a classic example of psychosomatic
healing. The paralytic had not handled his guilt
feelings, and some unresolved conflict had left him in a
spiritual straitjacket. Only when Jesus told him that his
sins were forgiven did he get up and walk. Jesus knew
that the body and spirit are one, and if either body or
spirit goes wrong, the other is affected.

In no way did Jesus mean to imply that sickness
was a way of God getting even with sinners, but he did
see a vital connection between sin and sickness. When
the man experienced God's freeing grace, his body also
became liberated.

The ancient Hebrews saw persons as a unit, and
for them it would be unthinkable to minister to the
body without ministering to the spirit. The Creation
stories in Genesis make clear that after God created
humans' physical bodies, God breathed into them the
breath of life.

Consider some of the following statements: "When Mary got hurt, I was worried sick." "Daddy didn't live much longer after Mother died. Sometimes I think he died of a broken heart." "Whenever I have to undergo medical tests, my hands begin to shake, and my heart is in my throat." "When we have an argument, I get butterflies in my stomach, even if he is a pain in the neck." All of these statements show the connectedness of mind, body, and spirit. Studies have shown that seventy-five percent of visits to doctors are either for illnesses that will ultimately get better by themselves or are related to stress. We can develop physical problems as a way of escaping from some stressful situation.

The paralytic had allowed his guilt to paralyze his life. His sickness removed him from responsibilities. He was so passive that he did not speak or act in the story *until* Jesus forgave his sins. Jesus saw beyond the paralysis of his body to his inner need.

Bill Moyers has said that we need a new medical paradigm that goes beyond "'body parts' medicine." Wholistic medicine is such a paradigm. Mind, soul, and body are interrelated, and health can only exist when they are in harmony.

Try this exercise. Spend a little time now in quiet prayer. If anything is making you anxious or nervous, try to let it go. Ask for God's grace. To symbolize the release of worry and fear, open your hands, palms up, on your lap. Feel the calm. Let God's healing power become real.

PRAYER
From every ailment flesh endures
Our bodies clamor to be freed;
Yet in our hearts we would confess
That wholeness is our deepest need.
(From "O Christ, the Healer" by Fred Pratt Green)

11

It Takes a Long Time to Bounce Back

READ PSALM 38

For I am ready to fall, and my pain is ever with me. . . . Do not forsake me, O LORD; O my God, do not be far from me. (Psalm 38:17, 21, NRSV)

ONE OF MY FAVORITE NURSERY RHYMES is the familiar tale of an egg named Humpty Dumpty:

> Humpty Dumpty sat on a wall,
> Humpty Dumpty had a great fall;
> All the king's horses,
> And all the king's men,
> Couldn't put Humpty together again.

Some recited this rhyme at the close of the Middle Ages about Richard III. He was the usurper of the English throne and he was not well liked. *Egg* was an insulting name used for a proud person in a precarious position. As Richard started to slip from the throne, even his supporters could not save his neck.

The author of Psalm 38 could have identified with Humpty. Some serious illness had caused a great fall. His pain was greater than he could describe. Like Humpty he asked the question, "What, when broken, can ever be repaired?" As any little child knows, when an egg is broken, it can never be put back again. We simply have to learn to live with the mess.

Recovering from surgery or any illness is not "a piece of cake." It is more like dealing with a broken egg. In my early days at home I wrote these words in my journal:

> No one ever warned me about the weariness and weakness I now feel. Certainly I have been sick before and have gone through surgery and its aftermaths. But I knew I would always get better. As the days wear on, a slow panic is seizing me and making me wonder, *Will I ever get better?* Sometimes I can't even remember what it was like to feel *well*.

Yet like the psalmist I prayed, "But it is for you, O Lord, that I wait; it is you, O LORD my God, who will answer" (Psalm 38:15, NRSV). I realized that even in my weakness, my soul was stronger.

A peasant lived in a village at the foot of a mountain range. In full view of the village on the side of the mountain stood a monastery. On one occasion a monk came to the village. The peasant ran and knelt before the monk, exclaiming, "O Father, surely yours is the best of all possible worlds, living so close to God in the clouds. What do you do up there?" The monk paused and then replied, "We fall down and we get up. We fall down and we get up. We fall down and we get up."

It does take a long time to bounce back from sickness. We want to be well *now*, and yet healing takes time.

STRENGTHENING GOD,
We know that life brings its ups and downs. Right now we feel broken and splattered on life's pavement. But you will not forsake us; God, see us through.
AMEN.

II

Surviving Job's Comforters

Caring has nothing to do with categories;

it shows the person that her life is valued

because it recognizes what makes her

experience particular. . . .

Care is inseparable from understanding,

and like understanding, it must be symmetrical. . . .

Caring for another, we either care for ourselves as well,

or we end in burnout and frustration.

ARTHUR W. FRANK

12

Miserable Comforters
READ JOB 16:1-6

*A despairing man should have the devotion of his friends,
. . . but my brothers are as undependable as intermittent
streams . . . miserable comforters are you all!*
(Job 6:14, 15; 16:2b, NIV)

I WILL NEVER FORGET VISITING A WOMAN who had just
returned from surgery. She was greeted by two self-ap-
pointed visitors from the church who sat perched by her
bedside for hours. Their presence was hardly appreciated at that time. The woman in pain opened her eyes,
glanced at the uninvited intruders, and muttered, "Job's
comforters!"

Job's world had fallen apart. He sat in misery on an
ash heap, the place where outcasts were required to go.
He had lost his livestock, his house, his children, and
even his health. He had lost everything and he was
asking the question, "Why?"

His three friends came to cheer him up, but their
words did more harm than good, for they were sure
that Job had done something terrible to deserve his
calamities. All he needed to do was confess his sin and
beg for forgiveness, and God would restore his
fortunes.

Frederick Buechner describes Job's friends in these
words:

They said that anybody with enough sense to come in out of the rain knew that God was just. They said that anybody old enough to spell his own name knew that since God was just, he made bad things happen to bad people and good things happen to good people.

So it was all too obvious that since bad things were happening to Job, he must have done bad things himself.

Playing the game of "blaming the victim," Job's friends stood firm that God makes no mistakes. It was Job's problem. But Job protested that there could be no connection between his faith and the enormous misfortunes that had come his way.

How could he reconcile a powerful, good God with his story? If God *was* God, God could not be good; and if God *was* good, in no way could God be God.

It is highly likely that anyone who experiences sickness will discover Job's comforters sooner or later. Some will imply that our sickness comes from our personal mistakes. Some may even tell us that we must have done something really bad, broken the laws of God and nature, or we wouldn't be sick. Granted, there are times when our unhealed stresses and unwise lifestyles can and do make us vulnerable to sickness. But seldom does sickness rise solely from our personal mistakes.

Watch out for Job's comforters, who speak pious platitudes often dressed in religious language but that make our lives miserable.

FRIEND OF EVERY SICK PERSON,
We know only too well our weakness and mistakes.
We don't need anyone to make us feel guilty.
What we crave in our sickness is your love and care.
AMEN.

Job's Friends Weren't All Bad
READ JOB 2:11-13

So they sat down with him on the ground seven days and seven nights, and no one spoke a word to him, for they saw that his grief was very great.
(Job 2:13, NKJV)

EVERYONE SEEMS TO BE HARD ON JOB'S friends, Zophar, Eliphaz, and Bildad. They were so preoccupied with their theology that they never really understood Job's pain. But they weren't all bad.

G. Campbell Morgan of London, England, wrote over forty years ago:

> For seven days they sat with him in silence. That is of the very essence of friendship. . . . They never spoke until he did. All they said was in answer to his first outpouring of grief, an outpouring made possible by their sublime and sympathetic silence.

That is a different slant on Job's comforters. His condition touched them to the depths, and for seven days and nights they sat with him *in silence.* What a blessing that must have been to Job.

Their presence and silence was a way they could let Job know they really did care. We all know moments of sorrow when friends and family surround us with love. No one says very much, for there isn't much to say. The silence of suffering is golden, then, but it can't last. Sooner or later someone has to speak, for the dreaded thing has happened. It was then that Job's friends attempted to get him to "come clean" and confess his hidden sins. That was the only way they could preserve their theology and rationalize what had happened to Job.

However, their early compassion and silence *is* a classic example of genuine caring. William B. Oglesby has well described genuine caring as

> a process whereby we listen with gentleness and patience, speak with truth and love, hold out a hand in time of loneliness and fear, sit in silence through the long night watches, and rejoice when the shadow of distress is dissolved in the warm sun of deliverance.

Job's friends offered that kind of care at first, but then they begin to blame him. As Arthur W. Frank says, "Job's friends appear as comforters, but they are really accusers." Perhaps we can learn a lesson from those friends. Silent presence may be the best care we can offer.

Take a moment if you are hospitalized or experiencing any illness, and reflect on friends and family members who have been there for you. And then breathe a silent prayer of thanksgiving for them.

LOVING GOD,
So often we cry to you, and there seems to be no answer.
Help us to realize that you are with us through the long night
watches, and you come to us through those who care.
AMEN.

Let Me Tell You about My Operation
READ PHILIPPIANS 2:1-4

*Out of humility of mind everyone should give
preference to others, everyone pursuing not selfish
interests but those of others.
(Philippians 2:3b, 4, NJB)*

YOU MAY HAVE HEARD OF THE PREACHER who had his
Sunday sermon on his mind when he visited a woman
who was recovering from a hysterectomy. Before she
could say a word he said, "Are you recovering from
your complete deuteronomy?" Too often people who
visit the sick are more preoccupied with their own
issues and bypass the feelings of the sick person.

The person we visit no sooner begins to talk about
themselves than we say, "Oh, yes, let me tell you about
my operation." While it may be helpful to show the
other person that he or she is not the only person in the
world who has been sick, this tactic does result in
blocking feelings. When the spotlight shifts to the
visitor, we lose the sick person.

When I had surgery, people inundated me with
war stories of their own surgeries or those of friends. I
never knew so many men had experienced prostate
surgery until I went through that older male's "rite of
passage." Hearing the grizzly details of someone who
had my problem and didn't do well is hardly any
comfort.

What we want when we go through sickness is someone who will be a good listener. Cabot and Dicks distinguish between passive and directed listening. Passive listening means we become a mirror, simply reflecting what the other person says. Without getting ourselves into the picture, we follow the person wherever he or she takes us. Directed listening means that we lead the person to think and talk about a certain subject.

As a result of my long recovery from surgery, surrounded by many visitors, if I had to choose my listener, I would prefer a passive listener. I am convinced that what we need when we are sick is to share our fears, anxieties, and concerns with another person. It would be best if we could do that with our physician, but that is not always possible.

People can usually solve their own problems and find the inner strength to get through crises if we let them talk things out and pray with them. No wonder Paul called Christians "ambassadors for Christ": "as though God were urging you through us" (2 Cor. 5:20, NJB). By the presence and loving concern of others, God comes to us.

I know one thing for sure. I will be a little slower from now on to talk about *my* operation when I am visiting the sick, and a little quicker to listen to their story.

MIGHTY COUNSELOR,
Thank you for being there when we need you and listening to our fears and complaints. And we remember now with thanksgiving family and friends who do hear us.
AMEN.

15

Funny Friends and Fidgety Relatives
READ JOB 42:10-17

Then there came to him all his brothers and sisters and all who had known him before, and they ate bread with him in his house; they showed him sympathy and comforted him . . . and each of them gave him a piece of money and a gold ring.
(Job 42:11, NRSV)

WHERE WERE JOB'S FAMILY AND FRIENDS when he really needed them? Were they ashamed of him or afraid his disease was contagious? When God restored Job's fortunes they all flocked to "comfort" him and shower him with their guilt gifts. Perhaps they finally came because of guilt feelings that they had let him down in his despair. Anyway, now it was safer to be present, since his disgrace had disappeared. But where were his family and neighbors with food and love when he *really* needed them?

I have always felt that the epilogue to the Book of Job raises serious questions. Does God always restore health to people with faith? Are we doubly blessed when we maintain our integrity? Does God always make things turn out with a happy ending? In that ancient culture Job's integrity had to be vindicated. By restoring Job's wealth and health, the author proves that Job's blunt accusations and protests were closer to the truth than his friends' theology.

It is significant that Job *is* changed. He prays for his friends and becomes their mediator. What a strange irony. It had been Job who on several occasions had begged God for a mediator, an umpire to plead his case and handle his conflict. Now Job becomes the mediator for his friends and prays for them.

Our fidgety relatives and funny friends may well feel guilty that they have not done enough for us, that they *ought* to be helping us more, that they *should* be of more assistance. What they need from us is acceptance. Myron Madden says,

> Whoever brings acceptance in a total way brings healing . . . a genuine self-acceptance must be started at some point outside the self; it must come from another self who has been able in turn to accept healing from his own brokenness.

Whether it be the sick person who offers that acceptance to family or friends or vice versa makes little difference. What does matter is that such acceptance frees people to accept themselves and find wholeness.

No one can force that acceptance. All we can do is take the initiative and wait for a response. We can knock at the door, but we must never violate a person's right to refuse our offer. We must be given power by the other to accept and heal.

Fidgety relatives and funny friends will try our souls. But our example is our Lord, who "when he was abused . . . did not return abuse; when he suffered, he did not threaten" (1 Pet. 2:23, NRSV).

STRENGTH OF THE WEAK,
*Can I dare to look beyond my own needs
and consider the needs of others?*
AMEN.

16

Those Mrs. Lincoln Responses
READ MARK 9:2-8

[Peter] did not know what to say, for they were terrified.
(Mark 9:6, NRSV)

PETER WAS SO OVERWHELMED BY THAT Transfiguration
experience that he didn't know what to say! Seeing
Moses and Elijah speaking with Jesus, basking in the
glory of that moment, was more than he could stand.
So, like most of us, he blurts out a response: "Rabbi, it is
good for us to be here; let us make three dwellings—
one for you, one for Moses, and one for Elijah." It was
hardly an appropriate remark in light of what Jesus
would reveal about his mission.

During my long convalescence, I became amused
at some of the remarks I heard from people. It
reminded me of what Brooke B. Collison calls "The Mrs.
Lincoln response": "Other than this, Mrs. Lincoln, how
did you enjoy the play?" Such remarks show a gross
insensitivity to the needs of others.

When my "friends" heard that I had suffered
through prostate surgery, that hushed-up malady of
older men, I heard the following Mrs. L. responses:

> "I don't know why you had such problems. My 85-
> year-old grandfather had that surgery, and he was
> chopping wood in two weeks!"

"Oh well, all you older men face that operation someday."

"Maybe you should have waited to see if there were some new techniques available, instead of rushing into surgery."

The classic Mrs. Lincoln response came from a woman who I knew was hypochondriac. She called and said, "I know exactly what you are going through. I had that surgery years ago, and I thought I would never recover from it." I even received a classic Mrs. L. response when I finally got out to church and one dear lady said, "Didn't you used to be Dick Morgan?"

No one can ever really understand what sickness means to a particular person. Every illness is unique. What we need are people who listen to us and truly care. Arthur W. Frank wisely says,

> I reserve the name "caregivers" for the people who are willing to listen to ill persons and to respond to their individual experiences. . . . When the caregiver communicates to the ill person that she cares about that uniqueness, she makes the person's life meaningful. And as that person's life story becomes part of her own, the caregiver's life is made meaningful as well.

It would have been better if Peter had practiced the old dictum, "silence is golden," and kept quiet. A short word of concern, a loving hug, and being willing to be there is the best caregiving a sick person needs.

GOD OF SILENCE,
Help us to offer our silent help when people hurt.
Teach us how to go beyond careless words to loving presence.
AMEN.

17

Whenever They Go
READ JOHN 16:1-7

*Still, I am telling you the truth: it is for your
own good that I am going.*
(John 16:7a, NJB)

ONE OF MY FRIENDS IS A CHARGE NURSE on a surgical
ward at our hospital, and she tells me that the worst
day for the nurses is Monday. Well, Monday usually *is*
the worse day of anyone's week, but her reason was
different. "On Monday we have to undo all the damage
the many visitors did to our patients on Sunday."

Jesus counseled the disciples that "it is for your
own good that I am going." That sounds strange, and
yet Jesus had to leave so that the Spirit might fill their
lives. Even though they would feel the pain of his
absence, they would later convert that pain into a
deeper understanding of his presence. Henri Nouwen
wisely says,

> In our ministry of visitation—hospital visits and
> home visits—it is essential for patients and
> parishioners to experience that it is good for them,
> not only that we come but also that we leave. . . . I am
> deeply convinced that there is a ministry in which
> our leaving creates space for God's Spirit and in
> which, by our absence, God can become present in a
> new way.

However, there is an enormous difference between an absence *after* a visit and an absence which is the result of *not coming at all*. There is a time to leave, but there is also a time to be present.

In my long days and weeks in the hospital and at home, I was intrigued by the different kinds of visits I experienced. The visit that really sticks in my mind was that of some former church members who came and sat and sat and sat. In my condition, sitting was most difficult. I stood up; they sat. I walked around the room; they talked on. Finally, in the nicest way possible, I asked them to leave. As the old saying goes, "Some people bring joy *wherever* they go; others *whenever* they go."

It is true in the spiritual realm too, that even God's seeming absence can become a creative space for God's presence. As the psalmist affirmed, "If I make my bed in Sheol [where God is not present], you are there" (Psalm 139:8*b*, NRSV).

ABSENT GOD,
When we hurt, we sometimes feel that you have left us.
We share the hurt of those first disciples when Jesus left them.
But now we know your absence can become a new space for
your presence.
AMEN.

18

Beyond the Medical Mystique
READ MARK 5:24-34

*Is there no balm in Gilead? Is there no physician
there? Why then is there no recovery for the health
of the daughter of my people?*
(Jeremiah 8:22, NKJV)

AUGUSTINE ONCE SAID THAT HE KNEW WHAT TIME was
until someone asked him. Most of us know what illness
is until someone asks us. Yet we are forever baffled and
bombarded by medical terms, what someone has called
"medicalese."

In the story of the woman with the hemorrhage,
Mark tells us that she "had suffered many things from
many physicians. She had spent all that she had, and
was no better, but rather grew worse" (Mark 5:26,
NKJV). Luke omits the part about her expensive and
unsuccessful treatment by doctors. Most scholars
believe that Luke transposed much of Mark's Gospel
into his own, adding his own material. Why, then, did
he omit the part about doctors? Luke is traditionally
identified as a physician; perhaps he did not like the
negative slurs on his profession!

All too often doctors use medical language to
explain our problems, sometimes not realizing that we
haven't the foggiest notion of what they are saying.
They even refer to us as "cases" and talk about
"procedures" and "prognoses." Nothing helps a person
who is sick more than a doctor who can talk plainly

with us. After all, it *is* our body, and we need to be assertive with doctors. Herbert Anderson says,

> The medical world needs to be demystified enough so that when we are patients, we are willing to insist on the information that is essential for responsible management of our illnesses or our treatment processes. Some physicians recognize that knowledgeable patients make better patients, others do not. But because of the mystique we attach to physicians, we hesitate asking them much.

I am one of those persons who wants to know about my illness. I used to attach a mystique to doctors and even perceive some as gods. No longer. Both before and after my surgery I bombarded my surgeon for information and an honest appraisal of my situation.

I admit that too much knowledge can be scary, but after suffering horrendous post-op complications I demanded to know why these mishaps occurred and what they meant. I am sure my doctor grew weary of my nagging questions, but I have a right to know and be involved in my healing process.

We are not "cases" but human beings. I am not some kind of a machine that can be "fixed" or corrected by a mechanic who goes under the hood to repair the damage, replace the parts, and revive the connections. I have feelings and concerns that doctors must not dismiss; they are powerful forces in my continued illness or my healing.

GOD OF TRUTH,
You don't hide anything from us if we want to know.
You speak the truth in love about our problems.
Give us grace to listen.
AMEN.

19

God's Strange Comfort
READ JEREMIAH 12:1-6

*If you have raced with men on foot and they have worn
you out, how can you compete with horses? If you
stumble in a safe country, how will you manage
in the thickets by the Jordan?*
(Jeremiah 12:5, NIV)

JEREMIAH WAS IN GREAT DIFFICULTY. He was already
unpopular and hated because of his warning that doom
was coming to the nation. Now he learned of a plot by
his neighbors at Anathoth to kill him. He takes his
complaint to God and asks, "Why does the way of the
wicked prosper? Why do all the faithless live at ease?"
(Jer. 12:1b) We might add, "Why am I, God's prophet,
suffering so?" He receives a strange answer.

He learns that it *will* get worse. Soon he will find
himself competing with cavalry and trying to survive in
the thickets by the Jordan. Yahweh is saying, "Jeremiah,
you ain't seen nothing yet!" Some comfort! No
assurance that things would get better, but blatant
announcement that they would get worse. What lay
ahead would make his present perils seem a "piece of
cake."

When we experience illness and cry out for
deliverance and healing, God doesn't always answer
that prayer. At times God seems distant in our distress,
and we begin to realize that harder days are ahead. In
my early convalescence, I recall pacing the floor and

begging God to be healed. Little did I realize the long, hard days that were ahead. I had thought that the surgery would be a "magic bullet" to cure all my problems, a quick fix for my discomfort. I soon realized that there would be long days and sleepless nights before healing could come. But Jeremiah discovered the strong comfort of God in those hard words. First, he learned that the difficulties of the past were intended to prepare him for the present . . . and future. As Nietzsche put it so well, "What doesn't destroy me strengthens me." The strength he had already won in conflict would prepare him for future battles. Secondly, Jeremiah learned that God had confidence in him and was entrusting him with even greater challenges in his future. Thus he learned to put his confidence in that God who stood with him and would remain with him.

We, too, ask God why our suffering seems so long. Like the ancient psalmist, we want God to even things up: "Let our joy be as long as the time that you afflicted us, the years when we experienced disaster" (Psalm 90:15, NJB).

A young man suffered seriously, and his surgery meant that his whole life had been shattered and changed. Yet, when I visited him in the hospital, he had a radiant faith and said to me, "I don't know why God has permitted this to happen to me. But I take heart that God entrusted this suffering to me. He must believe I can take it." I left his room humbled by his quiet faith and ashamed of my lack of trust.

STRONG COMFORTER,
You have never promised it would always turn out the way we expected. We may face even more difficult days. But we praise you for entrusting us with this sacred challenge.
AMEN.

20

Even the Worst Visit May Help
READ MATTHEW 15:21-28

*Jesus did not answer a word. So his disciples
came to him and urged him, "Send her away, for
she keeps crying out after us."
(Matthew 15:23, NIV)*

WHEN THE CANAANITE WOMAN VISITED JESUS and
begged for mercy for her sick daughter, she proved
quite a nuisance for the disciples. As Helen Bruch
Pearson described her, "Determined to get Jesus'
attention, she was a shouting, assaulting scene-maker of
the most irritating and embarrassing sort!" The
disciples even tried to chase her away.

Later on, however, when the woman persisted in
her faith and was commended by Jesus, the disciples
had to take a second look at this nuisance. This foreign
woman not only exposed their own prejudices but
extended the Lord's table to Gentiles.

One of my more thoughtful visitors in the hospital
perceived my discomfort and stayed only a few
minutes. She left me a copy of an excellent book, *Patient
Prayers: Talking to God from a Hospital Bed* (Crossroad,
1989), by John V. Chervokas. One of those prayers was
especially meaningful to me:

Prayer for a Well-Meaning Visitor
When I say "she means well"
the phrase probably says more about me
than it does about her.
And what it says about me
isn't all that flattering,
now is it, God?
Because when I say
"she means well"
it's always followed by
one of my critical "buts,"
as in:
"but she talks too much,"
"but she repeats herself,"
"but she doesn't know when to leave."
Help me to remember, dear God,
That the visitor *I* find tiresome,
You find a treasure;
The visitor *I* find boring,
You have blessed
just as wondrously
As *You* have blessed me.

I prayed that prayer many times in the hospital and at home. Yes, some of the visitors whom I found tiresome were treasures to God. Furthermore, I have learned to put myself in the place of the other person, and that makes a difference!

BOOK OF COMMON PRAYER
Keep watch, dear Lord, with those who work, or watch, or weep this night, and give your angels charge over those who sleep. Tend the sick, Lord Christ; give rest to the weary, bless the dying, soothe the suffering, pity the afflicted, shield the joyous; and all for your love's sake.
AMEN.

21

Someone Is *Waiting*
READ LUKE 15:11-32

But while he was still a long way off,
his father saw him and was filled with compassion for him;
he ran to his son, threw his arms around him and kissed him.
(Luke 15:20b, NIV)

HENRI NOUWEN TELLS THE STORY OF MR. HARRISON, a forty-eight-year-old farmer who faced surgery and was visited by a chaplain in the hospital. When asked if anyone was waiting for him when he leaves the hospital, he replied, "Nothing and nobody. Just hard work." Harrison died in surgery. Nouwen suggests that the chaplain could have said to him, "Look at me, and try to say that again . . . I am here, and I am waiting for you." Nouwen adds, "No man can stay alive when nobody is waiting for him. . . . A man can keep his sanity and stay alive as long as there is at least one person who is waiting for him."

What must have overwhelmed that younger son in Jesus' parable when he returned home was the sight of his old father waiting for him. "While he was a long way off, his father saw him. . . ." The father had been watching down the road for his son. His eyes had rested on that highway, always peering at the distant hills. When he saw him, he threw off all dignity and ran to shower his son with affection and love.

What does it mean that someone is waiting for us in that scary "waiting room" while we go through surgery? What does it mean that someone is waiting for us while we lie so helpless on a hard hospital bed or linger sick at home? *Everything in the world!* I recall how I experienced the same surgery twice, with vastly different results. The first time I went home to an empty, cold apartment. Nobody was there. I told myself, "I really am alone." It took weeks to regain even the semblance of health. The next time it was different. A caring wife was waiting. She had endured hours of waiting in the hospital and sat with me in my distress. And during the long weeks that ensued at home, she waited patiently, and constantly reassured me when I felt panic and dismay. It does make a big difference when there is someone who waits.

There is always Someone who waits. The father in the parable is Jesus' picture of God. God stands silently in hospital halls as we are wheeled into surgery. God waits while we struggle for healing. Every day and every cold winter night, God comes and stands with us and waits while we think that this life is only this sick bed and the pain of our illness.

Let us take heart. There are those people who wait for us and to whom we owe so much. But beyond them, God, the waiting father, comes to offer incredible healing and grace. A robe to cover our nakedness; shoes to show we are still his children; and a ring for healing and restoration.

GOD WHO WAITS,
Help us to truly believe that whatever happens to us,
You wait with love.
AMEN.

III

Going through the Valley of Baca

God whispers to us in our pleasures,

speaks in our conscience, but shouts in our pains:

it is His megaphone to rouse a deaf world.

C.S. LEWIS

22

This Lonesome Valley
READ PSALM 84

As they pass through the Valley of Baca,
they make it a place of springs.
(Psalm 84:6, NIV)

THE PSALMIST TELLS ABOUT GOD'S PEOPLE going through the Valley of Baca. This was a desolate valley, fit only for balsam trees. An arid, inhospitable area, it did serve as a route which travelers took on their way to Jerusalem. Since the word *Baca* is related in sound to the word *weep,* some have translated the phrase, "valley of weeping."

Although this valley was a difficult barrier on the way to Jerusalem, the pilgrim's anticipation of seeing the Temple transforms the desert into a place of springs. Thus "they go from strength to strength."

Sickness means we must go through the Valley of Baca. I know that the enforced inactivity and confinement of sickness was my Valley of Baca. I felt restless, anxious, and bored. Merril Morse has written,

> Healing, of course, takes time. . . . Affliction can be such a lonely experience. It is a valley through which each person must go alone. . . . No one else can step into our soul and feel exactly as we do.

Yet, this Valley of Baca can become a place of springs. As Isaiah declared, "Every valley shall be exalted, and every mountain and hill shall be made low; the crooked places shall be made straight, and the rough places smooth" (Isa. 40:4, NKJV).

Joseph Campbell is quoted as saying,

It is only by going down into the abyss / that we recover the treasures of life. / Where you stumble, / there lies your treasure. / The very cave you are afraid to enter / turns out to be the source of / what you are looking for.

My Valley of Baca became a place of springs. During my first days of discomfort and pain I wrote these words in my journal:

I am learning to be content, and the absence of any contact with the "outside world" has opened up a whole new world inside of me. My mind recalls when I was a boy of five, critically sick with pneumonia, in the days when no "miracle drugs" were available. I remember spending endless hours in a fantasy world, conquering giants and winning imaginary battles. Now I am fighting an even greater battle, trying to find a faith that will overcome the world.

Sickness means you enter a Valley of Baca, but it can become a place of springs! Let that thought be a comfort as you struggle through pain to growth.

———————

GOD OF HOPE,
Bring to us a renewed sense of hope,
that we may be able to pass through the valleys of sickness
to the springs of health.
AMEN.

23

Those In-Between Times
READ JEREMIAH 29:1-14

Therefore do not worry about tomorrow,
for tomorrow will worry about itself.
Each day has enough trouble of its own.
(Matthew 6:34, NIV)

MOST OF LIFE IS LIVED IN THE MEANTIME. Never is this truer than when we are sick. Our illness forces us into long periods of delay, and we feel life is "on hold." This in-between time frustrates us. We live in an age of the instantaneous; we're accustomed to fast results. Computers yield immediate answers. Fax machines, space travel, and other marvels of technology make us believe that "faster *is* better."

Jeremiah's letter to the exiles in Babylon dealt with the issue of life in the meantime. Despite their anxiety about their future, he cautioned them to be patient. His counsel was simply this: "You are going to be here for some time to come. Settle in, learn to live with it, and do whatever you can to improve your life where you are. Give it your best and you will find peace." They were 900 miles and a thousand days from home, but they had to find courage to accept life as it was.

Sickness usually forces us to live in a strange limbo between life as it was and an unknown future. It is a difficult time, and our patience often wears thin. We want healing *now*, without waiting for God's time.

Jesus admonished his disciples, "Do not be anxious about tomorrow." He warns not against common sense foresight but against crippling anxiety about the future. He does not rule out concern for the future or sanction a whatever-will-be resignation. But he warns against an *anxious* concern for the future, the kind of concern that keeps us from enjoying the present moment.

Whenever sickness comes to us, we may slip over into disabling anxiety. How long will it take to feel better? Will I ever get over the lingering effects of the surgery? Why can't I bounce back as quickly as I used to? So the in-between times become anxious times.

In a sermon, Karl Barth once said,

> God always gives us strength for one leg of the journey at a time. At each stage we are promised that he will continue to provide additional and greater strength as needed on our way into the future. . . . God does not distribute the full ration at once. He apportions it from one day to the next.

So in this in-between time, when the future is not yet and the past is still focal in our mind, let us live today and trust God for tomorrow.

GOD WHO STANDS BY US,
Forgive our feverish concern over the future,
and give us grace to live this day
in simple trust and quiet confidence.
AMEN.

24

When You Are Reminded of Your Surgery
READ JOSHUA 3:1-6

*"You have never gone this way before.". . . Joshua said to the
people, "Sanctify yourselves; since tomorrow Yahweh will
work wonders among you."*
(Joshua 3:4-5, NJB)

ONE OF THE STRANGE PHENOMENA that can happen to a
person recovering from surgery is flashbacks of the
surgery experience. The marvels of modern anesthesia
remove most memories of that experience, and the
actual event is blocked from our consciousness.

Yet, I discovered in the first weeks of being at
home that memories of the surgery experience came
back to me. It seemed as if I needed to relive the
moment and process its meaning.

Entering surgery is a frightening experience. One
of the loneliest moments in our lives comes the night
before surgery. The waiting is the worst part, especially
if you are "bumped" and wait for hours. You enter the
operating room on a gurney, your identity reduced to a
surgery gown and a plastic band on your wrist. You are
totally out of control, with virtually every aspect of your
life in the hands of others.

I recall thinking about how the Israelites must have
felt when they prepared to cross the Jordan River and
enter an unknown land. They must have been terrified.
But Joshua said to them, "You have never gone this

way before. Sanctify yourselves; since tomorrow Yahweh will work wonders among you."

Facing surgery is like crossing the Jordan River. It is a visible barrier between the patient and a new life of promise; it is a time to consecrate oneself to God. Too often we fill our minds with fears and anxieties as we enter surgery, instead of thinking about wonders and blessings God may have for us after surgery.

I confess that my prayers before surgery were more for deliverance from danger than praying for strength to meet any new challenges. It *is* a new and often threatening experience. But it is also a time to experience God's grace.

Recently I was saying good-bye to a woman who had undergone successful surgery and was on her way home. As they wheeled her out of the hospital into the warm sun of a summer day, she said, "Now on to a new life after surgery." She captured what Joshua meant. Beyond the Jordan, beyond surgery, God is present with new challenges and wonders, and we can be confident that "the One who began a good work in [us] will go on completing it until the Day of Jesus Christ comes" (Phil. 1:3, NJB).

It helped me to remember those moments . . . the night before surgery, the interminable delay, the awesome loss of control. God does go before us and prepare the way.

———

EVER-PRESENT GOD,
Give us confidence when we
go through the unknown land of surgery. Give us
trust in your presence, and healing of memories.
AMEN.

25

Escaping into Sickness?
READ JOHN 5:1-9

*When Jesus saw him lying there and learned that he had been
in this condition for a long time, he asked him,
"Do you want to get well?"
(John 5:6, NIV)*

THIS UNNAMED MAN HAD BEEN SICK for thirty-eight
years, waiting for someone to put him into the pool of
Bethesda. The pool was a gathering place for invalids
from all over the country who lay under the shadow of
the five porches. Legend said that from time to time an
angel stirred the waters, and when that happened,
whoever got into the pool first would be healed. The
sight of such a crowd of sick people must have
awakened the compassion of Jesus, but he singled out
this man.

Jesus asked him what appeared to be an
insensitive and crazy question, *"Do you want to get
well?"* Surely this man wanted to get well, or why had
he come to the healing waters? The question seemed
hardly consistent with the gentleness Jesus had shown
to other sick persons. Perhaps Jesus knew that this man
struggled with the idea of being well. As a sick person,
little was expected of him. Some kind souls had to feed
and clothe him and carry him to the pool every day. If
he got well, he would have to take care of himself.

Kenneth Pelletier says that many people escape
from stressful situations by getting sick.

He makes an unconscious choice, which allows him a means of coping with this irresolvable situation. One means of resolution is to develop a psychosomatic disorder. . . . These symptoms allow an individual to remove himself from an untenable situation when he cannot extricate himself by any other means.

Notice Jesus does not feed the man's self-pity. Jesus confronts him. For healing is more than physical restoration; it means a radical change of life.

Jesus, the Great Physician, knew that the man really did want to get well, so he said, "Get up! Pick up your mat and walk." And the man began a new life. Later, Jesus sought out the man and said, "You are well again. Stop sinning or something worse may happen to you." Getting well put him into the greatest jeopardy of his life. He had to give up his dependence on others and become responsible for himself. We can surmise that his whole life changed from demanding selfishness to productive usefulness.

There is nothing wrong with the need for extra care. The wrong comes when we use illness as an excuse for acting more helpless than we actually are. Jesus confronts us with the timeless question, "Do you want to get well?" And we choose whether we prefer escaping into sickness or becoming responsible to life.

SUSTAINER OF LIFE,
Help us to want to be well, despite the cost.
Forgive us for using our sicknesses as a way
to refuse your call to life and commitment.
AMEN.

26

Dealing with Guilt
READ JOHN 9:1-12

*"Neither this man nor his parents sinned," said Jesus,
"but this happened so that the work of God
might be displayed in his life."*
(John 9:3, NIV)

THE STORY OF THE MAN BORN BLIND is filled with people
who ask questions. His neighbors want to know how he
received his sight. The Pharisees wonder who this Jesus
is, who restored the man's sight. But the disciples'
question haunts us when we are sick. "Who sinned?"
Whose fault is it: his, or his parents'?

Guilt always stalks the path of people who are
sick. Sick people torture themselves with questions like,
"Why didn't I see a doctor earlier?" or "Why didn't I
get more information on my problem and save myself
some real pain?" We also feel guilty about being extra
burdens for our family. Their lives are stressed enough
without having to deal with our sickness.

Even when we get better, we sometimes experience
"survivor guilt" when we realize how many others are
not as fortunate as we. A friend said to me, "It's great to
see someone doing well." That evoked some real guilt
as I thought about many who are not so fortunate and
are not doing well.

I confess that I experienced some guilt when I gave
up my work with a church after surgery. My guilt was
exacerbated by the fact that the church was still working

through its guilt over the suicide of a former pastor, and I was needed there. I sometimes wondered if my sickness was not a punishment for the way I had failed that church.

The story of the man born blind brought comfort. In no way was there a straight line between the man's blindness and anyone's sin. Rather, it became an opportunity for God to move into the life of a person, bringing wholeness.

Wayne Muller writes,

> When we seek to blame, we distract ourselves from an exquisite opportunity to pay attention, to see even in this pain a place of grace, a moment of spiritual promise and healing.

Do not torture yourself with guilt that you did something to cause your sickness. Instead, let your illness become an opportunity for "a moment of grace" in your life.

Sickness is not being beaten up by God but an opportunity for promise and healing. Its cause may be inexplicable, yet it can become the moment when God brings wholeness into your life. The man born blind began to live a different life not only because he could now see but also because he recognized Jesus as the light of the world. That light scatters our darkness and removes our guilt.

LIGHT OF OUR LIVES,
May your healing light flood our souls,
reminding us that our sickness is not punishment
but an opportunity for growth.
AMEN.

27

At My Wit's End
READ PSALM 107

They were at their wit's end.
Then they cried out to the Lord in their trouble,
and he brought them out of their distress.
(Psalm 107:27b-28, NIV)

HISTORIAN SHELBY FOOTE TELLS OF A SOLDIER who was wounded at the battle of Shiloh during the American Civil War and was ordered to go to the rear. The fighting was fierce, and within minutes he returned to his commanding officer. "Captain, give me a gun!" he shouted. "This fight ain't got any rear."

There are times during prolonged illness when you do feel pressured on every side, at your wit's end. The writer of Psalm 107 had reached his wit's end. In this psalm we read a vivid description of sailors caught in a violent storm at sea that tossed their frail ship like a toy. With all their nautical skill and experience, they felt helpless. They were at their wit's end.

No doubt the disciples of Jesus felt the same panic that night on the Lake of Galilee, when they struggled against the wind and waves and were making little progress.

Yet in both stories God came to deliver. The psalmist witnesses to the fact that when the sailors cried to the Lord, "he brought them out of their distress, and stilled the storm to a whisper." Jesus came to the disciples in their distress and brought deliverance.

During my sickness, there were times when I reached my wit's end. I felt like a wounded, old dog who had suffered a resounding defeat at the hands of a younger foe and crawled home, looking for some sanctuary where he could lick his wounds. It wasn't only the discomfort and weakness but my faith questions. Why did *I* have to be in the 1.5 percent of patients who suffer these complications? Why couldn't I have breezed through this surgery like other men? Was I being punished for some hidden sin?

What I learned was that sometimes we have to experience how bad things are before we can experience God's presence. After all, some of the holiest people have suffered the most. God does not send sickness, or spare anyone. God stands with us when we reach our wit's end.

William B. Ward, in his priceless book *The Divine Physician*, tells the legend of a young man who went with an old violin maker into the forest to cut wood for violins. They passed through the fertile valley and went high on the crags of the mountainside, where gnarled and knotted trunks were twisted by gales. The boy asked why they had not stopped in the valley below, where the trees grew straight and tall. The old violin maker explained how the wood which grew up quickly in the sheltered valley would break under the strain of being made into violins; but the trees that all their lives had been lashed and torn by the gales were tough, and when carved into violins made the sweetest music.

GOD OF MANY DELIVERANCES,
We feel at times that we are being torn and tossed
by storms and distress. But you will deliver us.
AMEN.

28

Learning in God's Night School
READ 1 SAMUEL 3:1-10

Wearisome nights have been appointed to me. When I lie down, I say, "When shall I arise, and the night be ended?" For I have had my fill of tossing till dawn.
(Job 7:3b-4, NKJV)

LIKE MANY SICK PEOPLE, JOB SUFFERED from sleepless nights. He knew what it was like to face the long darkness and the unending tossing and turning. Sleepless nights may accompany recovery from surgery. Inactivity brings disturbance to sleep patterns.

At times I became anxious, even resentful about losing sleep. Then I remembered the Bible story from childhood, how God called Samuel in a sleepless night. At first Samuel thought it was Eli who called him; later he realized it was God, who neither slumbers nor sleeps, whose voice he heard.

Sleepless nights can become *God's night school.* When we realize this, even "tossing and turning" can become moments of grace. Many people suffer from such times, but few realize that these hours can become a spiritual opportunity. We need to accept this "friendly silence" as a time to listen for God's call in the darkness. In time I began to turn away from late television watching and looked at those hours as "found time," a time for meditation and prayer.

Although at first Samuel mistook the voice for that of his old mentor, eventually he made a simple affirmation of trust. "Speak, Lord, for thy servant hears." I recall from childhood how I identified with the boy Samuel, who must have been awestruck when God spoke to him. I wondered what I might do under similar circumstances should the voice of God call me in the night. I have received no startling revelation, but I am learning in God's night school.

I used some of the "found time" for recreational reading, especially biographies long neglected in my wakeful life. Nighttime was also an opportunity to listen to music or other recordings. At times I lay in the darkness and reminisced, recalling moments I wanted to relive in the wonderful world of fantasy. I believe my "right brain" was turned on in these hours when everything was so still. Some of the time I prayed and asked God's blessings on family and friends.

Paradoxically, giving myself the freedom to *use* my wakefulness often helped me drift into sleep, instead of fretting, "I am wide awake." Viktor Frankl wrote,

The fear of sleeplessness results in a hyper-intention to fall asleep, which, in turn, incapacitates the patient to do so. To overcome this particular fear, I usually advise the patient not to try to sleep but rather to try to do just the opposite, that is, to stay awake as long as possible.

GOD OF THE LONG NIGHT WATCHES,
Make me hear in the shadows of the night your voice,
which so often I stifle in the frenzy of the day.
AMEN.

29

Depleted Strength/Defiant Spirit
READ 2 CORINTHIANS 12:1-9

Have pity on me, Yahweh, for I am fading away.
Heal me, Yahweh, my bones are shaken,
my spirit is shaken to its very depths.
(Psalm 6:2, NJB)

THE WRITER OF THIS PSALM HAD EXPERIENCED some life-shattering distress, probably a serious sickness. His strength was depleted, "fading away," and his whole life, body and spirit, was shaken to its very depths.

Many times in my convalescence I felt an incredible weakness. It takes time to recover from surgery, regain strength, and return to health. We still live in a culture which tells us to avoid pain and deny weakness. "I haven't got time for the pain," asserts one of the advertising slogans for a particular brand of pain-killing medication.

Going through the pain, getting in touch with weakness, is part of the process of healing. Paul learned this truth when he prayed for strength and was told by God, "Your strength is made perfect in weakness." That brought a measure of comfort to me during those difficult days of depleted strength. Paul Tournier wisely says,

> The strength which comes from God can heal, it can give strength to the weak, but that is only one aspect of its power. It does much more; it saves and

quickens. . . . Yes, sometimes the grace which comes from God—his grace—heals; sometimes it lifts us out of our weakness; but sometimes, too, it leaves our weakness with us, and gives us a quite different strength—the strength to accept it.

At the moment when my strength was depleted, I felt my spirit was defiant. My prayer was for strength to accept my weakness.

I admit there were times when I thought I would never get better and my strength might never return. I edged ever closer to final despair. Then I recalled the story of Shadrach, Meshach, and Abednego who told the king that their God was able to deliver them from his blazing furnace, "but even if he does not . . . we will not serve your gods" (Dan. 3:18, NIV). At that point I confessed my fear that the rest of my life might mean debility and weakness. But even if that be my lot, I would not surrender to despair or give up the struggle.

An African prayer became a daily companion:

O Lord, Creator,
Ruler of the world, Father,
I thank, thank, thank you
that you have brought me through.
How strong the pain was—
but you were stronger.
How deep the fall was—
but you were even deeper.
How dark was the night—
but you were the noonday sun in it.
You are our father,
our mother,
our brother and our friend.
Your grace has no end,
and your light no snuffer.

30

Unanswered Prayers
READ 2 CORINTHIANS 12:1-9

I was given a thorn in the flesh . . .
About this, I have three times pleaded with the Lord
that it might leave me, but he answered me,
"My grace is enough for you:
for power is at full stretch in weakness."
(2 Corinthians 12:7a, 8, 9, NJB)

PAUL HAD SOME PHYSICAL PROBLEM that plagued his life. He prayed for relief. He begged the Lord to rid him of this pain. Each time he prayed he got the same answer, "My grace is enough for you." He did not get *his* prayer answered. He did not receive physical healing. He was not relieved of his pain; he was not made well. But he did receive grace; he was made strong.

There were times during my sickness that I felt my prayers for healing were not answered. I wondered why God didn't do something about my pain. I felt abandoned. Although I knew people were caring *for* me, I still felt that no one really cared *about* me. Even God seemed distant and aloof.

We tend to waltz through life until some threat disrupts our comfortable living and becomes the main focus of our existence. And, with Martha of Bethany we cry out, "Lord, if you had been here . . ."

I have heard many answers given to this persistent problem of unanswered prayer: that God doesn't make exceptions for good people; that suffering refines character; that love is costly and never without pain. But they all seem so glib when you hurt and pray for deliverance, and the heavens seem like brass.

I have learned that when everything goes well in our lives, God is an interruption. When life tumbles in, God is a necessity. We learn with Paul that God's everlasting arms *are* underneath when life closes in. We may not be promised relief from the pressures, but we are given sufficient grace.

Larry Dossey says,

> Sickly saints and healthy sinners show us that there is no invariable, linear, one-to-one relationship between one's level of spiritual attainment and the degree of one's physical health. It is obvious that one can attain immense spiritual heights and still get *very* sick.

When the thorn is not removed, and our prayers seem unanswered, we may be surprised to discover that this becomes the moment for sharpened awareness of God's grace. Let our prayer echo that of Richard of Chichester from the twelfth century:

> *Thanks be to thee,*
> *Lord Jesus Christ,*
> *for all the benefits*
> *which thou hast won for us,*
> *for all the pains and insults*
> *which thou hast borne for us.*
> *O most merciful Redeemer,*
> *Friend and Brother,*
> *may we know thee more clearly,*
> *love thee more dearly,*
> *and follow thee more nearly,*
> *day by day.*

31

Mr. Bell's Mixed Blessing
READ ECCLESIASTES 3:1-7

For everything there is a season, and a time for every matter under heaven. . . . A time to keep silence, and a time to speak.
(Ecclesiastes 3:1,7b, NRSV)

ANYONE WHO EXPERIENCES LONG PERIODS OF recovery from sickness at home appreciates Alexander Graham Bell's invention of the telephone. We tend to forget that this discovery grew out of Bell's concern for teaching visible speech to people who were deaf. It is a valuable asset to recovery when you are confined at home or need a word of reassurance.

However, it can also be a problem, when well-meaning friends talk too much. Michel Quoist's prayer expresses this problem in powerful words,

> I have just hung up;
> why did he telephone?
> I don't know. . . . Oh! I get it. . . .
> I talked a lot and listened very little.
> . . . .
> Forgive me, Lord; for we were connected,
> And now we are cut off.

As the writer of Ecclesiastes said so well, "There is a time to keep silent . . ." and concerned friends and relatives should do more listening than talking when they call. I have learned to steer my friends in a direction so that they will soon hang up when they phone and get too wordy. I usually say, "Let me tell you some of the gory details of my operation," and they cut off quickly.

Thich Nhat Hanh, a Buddhist monk, claims that the ring of a telephone *may* be a "bell of mindfulness." He says, "Think *This sound brings me back to myself.* Then the ring of the phone can bring you peace and love, and when you answer it, you will be in a different place. The call becomes a gift."

I realized that truth in another way, when two calls asked for *my* help. One was a disabled minister who needed help in getting financial assistance. The other was a minister who was disheartened because he could not make a career move. The "bell of mindfulness" became the awareness that I could still be a helper to someone, even though confined at home and temporarily removed from the mainstream of life. Although I was not ready to get back into my role as a helper, those calls became symbolic of a future day when I would return to "active service."

On a deeper level, one of our problems in conversation with God is that we bombard heaven with our words and speech, instead of listening for that "still, small voice." We can also pray, "Forgive me, Lord, for we were connected and are now cut off." We need to hear the word God spoke to Jeremiah, "Call to me and I will answer you, and will tell you great and hidden things that you have not known" (Jer. 33:3, NRSV).

Let us listen quietly for God.

32

Clipped Wings/Growing Soul
READ JOHN 15:1-5

A man's spirit sustains him in sickness,
but a crushed spirit who can bear?
(Proverbs 18:14, NIV)

ONE OF THE REMARKS I RECALL FROM THE EARLY days of my sickness was, "Your wings have really been clipped!" Yes, there were times when I felt like a bird whose wings had been clipped. I was slowed down, restricted to two rooms.

Jesus says to the disciples that although they are related to him as branches are related to a vine, they still need to be pruned to bear more fruit. Pruning means cutting, clipping, reshaping, and removing what diminishes life. From my bedroom window I watched my wife pruning bushes and became fearful that they would never be green again. It is only later that we realize that pruning enables plants to produce more blossoms than they ever could, had they remained unpruned.

Henri Nouwen captures the spiritual meaning of Jesus' words about the vine and branches when he says,

> Grateful people are those who can celebrate even the pains of life because they trust that when the harvest comes the fruit will show that the pruning was not punishment but purification. I am gradually learning that the call to gratitude asks us to say, "Everything is grace." God does purify us through pain.

I recall reading about an Eskimo sculptor who always began his work on a fresh chunk of soapstone by pausing and asking, "I wonder what shape is hiding in this stone?" He saw his skill as listening for the whispered message of the figure that already existed in the stone. He had to be patient enough to wait for instructions on how it might be liberated.

Sickness is a graceful pause, a time to listen to what God is saying to us in this "unformed time." The words *nowhere* and *now here* have the same arrangement of letters; what separates them is a small space in the latter. Likewise, a fine space separates us from experiencing life as *nowhere* or *now here*.

The writer of Proverbs makes it clear. "A man's spirit sustains him in sickness; but a crushed spirit who can bear?" Waiting with clipped wings is never easy. But it can be a time of real growth. Søren Kierkegaard said, "When a man suffers and is willing to learn from suffering then he constantly learns about himself and his relationship to God. This is a sign he is being trained for eternity."

LORD OUR GOD,
Thou knowest our sorrow better than we know it ourselves....
Whatever care thou dost inflict upon us,
let us receive it from thy hand with humility
and give us the strength to bear it.
(Prayer of Kierkegaard)

IV

Spiritual Support for Scary Times

There is a healing force within each of us,

a kind of divine physician seated within our minds

and in communication with every cell of our being. . . .

The experience of illness is a call to

a genuinely religious life. In that sense,

it is for many people one of the best things

that ever happened to them.

MARIANNE WILLIAMSON

33

Supportive Friends
READ ECCLESIASTICUS 6:13-17

You are those who have stood by me in my trials.
(Luke 22:28, NRSV)

SUPPORTIVE FRIENDS ARE REAL TREASURES when one is sick. Ben Sira said it well, "A loyal friend is a powerful defense; whoever finds one has indeed found a treasure" (Ecclesiasticus 6:14, NJB). All too often friends appear and then vanish when sickness lingers. Stanley Hauerwas comments,

> For often we are willing to be present and sympathetic with someone with an intense but temporary pain—that is, we are willing to be present as long as they work at being "good" sick people who try to get well quickly and do not make too much of their discomfort. . . . It seems to be asking too much of us to be compassionate year in and year out.

Jesus thanked the disciples for being friends who stuck with him through his trials.

It takes commitment and love to care. We need only recall the four friends of the paralyzed man who carried him to Jesus. Not being able to get near Jesus, they climbed to the flat roof of the house and lowered their friend through the roof so that he was lying right at the feet of Jesus. The text tells us that when Jesus saw *their* faith (the faith of the friends), the man was healed.

Henri Nouwen describes a supportive friend:

The friend who can be silent with us in a moment of despair or confusion, who can stay with us in an hour of grief and bereavement, who can tolerate not-knowing, not-curing, not-healing and face with us the reality of our powerlessness, that is the friend who cares.

Because medical staff are preoccupied with diagnosis and treatment, they cannot provide care-giving. Their concern is with the disease, not the illness. So they usually have little time or inclination for listening to the needs of the sick person. But members of the family tend to perceive, respond, and live with the inner needs of the sick person. On them the real burden falls.

During the long, difficult hours of illness and the struggle back to health, we praise God for friends and family who stand by us in our trials. Their non-anxious presence, genuine concern, and availability make the road to recovery much easier. The ancient proverb says it best, "Some friends play at friendship but a true friend sticks closer than one's nearest kin" (Prov. 18:24, NRSV).

A PRAYER OF JOHN CALVIN

May we be so bound up in love with those for whom we pray,
that we may feel their needs as acutely as our own,
and intercede for them with sensitivity, with understanding,
and with imagination. We ask this in Christ's name.
AMEN.

34

Treasure in Scripture
READ LUKE 24:13-35

Your word is a lamp to my feet and a light for my path.
(Psalm 119:105, NIV)

DURING THE LONG DAYS AND NIGHTS of being bedfast and immobilized, I will never forget how I remembered scriptures that I had memorized from childhood. As a child I had been taught by my parents to "hide God's word in my heart," and now those precious words returned.

I remembered memorizing the Sermon on the Mount as a boy and reciting it before the congregation. Jesus' words about anxiety and the Father's care now became real, and I thanked God that I had been "soaked in the scriptures."

An explorer discovered an ancient sundial. Recognizing its value, he restored it to its original condition and put it in a museum where it would be shielded from the elements—including the sun! Although he valued it, he never used it. Many Christians do the same with the Bible. It is valued and cherished and remains the best seller. But it is *not* read or used. That is as strange as if every home should have a television set and never turn it on.

Two men in Africa were working side by side. One was a missionary engaged in translating the Bible. The other was an African called in by the missionary to check his translation. The African was unfamiliar with much of the Bible, and so the missionary would stop from time to time to make sure the translations were clear. Suddenly the African said, "This book is not like other books. When a man reads this book, he hears another speaking to him in his heart."

Rereading the Psalms as a sick person, I began to recognize my story in these songs of faith, and the Bible "came alive" in a new way.

Like the psalmist, I heard those who thought "he has taken to his bed and will never get up again" (Psalm 41:8*b*). I could resonate with "my strength has ebbed away. . . . My friends shun me in my sickness" (Psalm 38:10). The words of Psalm 88 (verses 3, 4, 8*b*) seemed written about me: "For my soul is full of trouble and my life draws near the grave. . . . I am like a man without strength. . . . I am confined and cannot escape."

I realized that their experience mirrored mine, and although they (and I) experienced no quick fix to our sickness, we did find a new sense of the presence of God. No wonder the writer of Psalm 23 finds God most personal ("Thou art with me") in the dark valleys.

The two persons on the Emmaus walk found a living word for their despair as Jesus explained the scriptures. "Were not our hearts burning within us as he talked to us on the road and opened the Scriptures to us?" (Luke 24:32, NIV) Despair became hope as words became living words. Those of us who are ill can find ourselves in these pages and—what is even more—can find a living faith!

LIVING WORD,
In our sickness may we discover your word as a
lamp to our feet and a light to our path.
AMEN.

35

Intentional Prayer
READ MATTHEW 6:6-9

*But when you pray, go to your private room, shut yourself in,
and so pray to your Father who is in that secret place,
and your Father who sees all that is done in secret
will reward you.*
(Matthew 6:6, NJB)

I AM SURE I COULD HAVE ECHOED the disciples' request of Jesus, "Lord, teach us to pray." Like them, I have prayed since childhood yet so often never *really* prayed. When they heard Jesus pray, they knew the poverty of their own prayer life. Whether lying down on a hospital bed or at home, we are forced to look up. When pain persists and we become frantic about our slow recovery, we are driven to our knees in prayer.

This truth came home to me with powerful impact in a moment of despair. My condition seemed worse, the bleeding continuing, so I called my surgeon to make sure my situation was "normal." It baffles me that doctors leave us in the dark as to what is "normal" after surgery. Although his nurse reassured me, I was still anxious. I recall kneeling down beside a chair in my bedroom, as the warm sunlight streamed through the window onto my face, and really praying. At first my condition did not improve, but my attitude did. There is little doubt that prayer changes *us*!

Augustine said that our prayers have a voice of their own quite apart from our voice. As Paul wrote, "In the same way, the Spirit helps us in our weakness. We do not know what we ought to pray for, but the Spirit ... intercedes for us with groans that words cannot express" (Rom. 8:26, NIV). That late autumn afternoon I knew the Spirit was praying in me.

Ann and Barry Ulanov describe the ways in which God hears our prayers: "God hears all the voices that speak out of us—our vocal prayer, the prayer said in our minds, the unvoiced longing rising from our hearts, the many voices of which we are not conscious but which cry out." God heard my cries and broken words.

Nothing means more to persons experiencing sickness than prayer. We pray as we enter the unknown world of surgery; we pray as we wait to be dismissed from the hospital; we pray when healing seems to take so much time and struggle. My prayers became intentional when I had nowhere else to turn. God heard me and brought peace.

One of the prayers that helped me later was a prayer by Leslie Weatherhead. Make this *your prayer* now.

For all sufferers for whom the lonely hours pass so very slowly on leaden feet; who wonder in the dawn however they will get through the day, and who all through the endless night, look at the time again and again, wonder whether the dark hours will ever pass; . . . for all such we pray that they may find the courage they need. AMEN.

36

Winter Spirituality
READ PSALM 30

I will extol you, O LORD, for you have drawn me up,
and did not let my foes rejoice over me.
O LORD my God, I cried to you for help,
and you have healed me.
(Psalm 30:1-2, NRSV)

ONE WISE COMMENT MY SURGEON MADE to me after the operation was, "Slow down. Recovery takes time. This is a good time to meditate." At first I bristled at this advice, but later I realized the wisdom of his words. Enforced inactivity after surgery is a kind of winter, a slowdown of life.

The writer of Psalm 30 had been through some horrendous winters in his life. He was about to die with a serious illness, but God heard his cry and brought him up from the realm of the dead into which he was sinking as his life ebbed away. God had turned his "mourning into dancing" and restored him to health.

I wrote in my journal during these days,

Now as I write these words I watch the fall of autumn leaves, striking the earth. Just as nature sheds its leaves as winter comes, so we must be stripped of the "dead weights" of our lives, so we can grow in grace. I see the wisteria outside the window, whose bright, green leaves are now becoming yellow with the advent of winter. But hope springs eternal that spring will bring new life. So with illness.

Marianne Williamson shows how illness can be a time of spiritual renewal.

> One of the problems with illness is that it strongly tempts us to obsess about the body at the very time when we need most to concentrate on the spirit. It takes spiritual discipline to turn that around.

Sickness is winter time, with its chilly messages of enforced silence and reminder of death. Joan Borysenko in her book *Fire in the Soul* writes, "Dark nights of the soul are extended periods of dwelling at the threshold when it seems as if . . . there is nothing familiar left to hold onto that can give us comfort."

Winter is a time to slow down, regroup, and recharge our spiritual batteries. Enforced inactivity caused by illness can mean "winter grace," as we take time for our souls. Annie Dillard described this in *Pilgrim at Tinker Creek:* "I bloom indoors in the winter like a forced forsythia; I come in to come out." Just as forces are at work in nature that bring spring after winter, so God's healing is at work in our winters of sickness.

***

A PRAYER OF BEETHOVEN

We must praise your goodness that you have left nothing undone to draw us to yourself. But one thing we ask of you, our God, not to cease to work for our improvement. Let us tend toward you, no matter by what means, and be fruitful in good works, for the sake of Jesus Christ our Lord.
AMEN.

37

What Julian of Norwich Taught Me
READ ROMANS 8:35-39

No, in all these things we are more than conquerors
through him who loved us.
(Romans 8:37, NIV)

ONE OF THE SAINTS OF THE CHRISTIAN church whom I discovered through spiritual reading in my convalescence was Julian of Norwich. She lived a contemplative life in cell-like quarters near the parish church of Norwich, England.

At the age of 30, Julian experienced a severe illness. On May 8, 1373, her illness reached a crisis. Neither she nor those who surrounded her bed thought she could survive, and three days before her mystic experience the priest had administered final rites. The priest held a crucifix before her eyes and said, "I have brought you the image of your saviour. Look at it and take comfort from it."

About four o'clock in the morning, as dawn was breaking, she received sixteen mystic revelations, *showings*, which she later recorded as *Revelations of Divine Love.* Her health was remarkably restored, and her experience of God's love is timeless.

She wrote, "All shall be well, and all shall be well, and all manner of thing shall be well." When Julian spoke these words she did *not* mean, of course, that in the short run everything will be well in the sense that we shall be spared suffering, anxiety and all the other pains which afflict us. We will be delivered *through* trials, not *from* them. For a sick person, struggling with the uncertainty of the healing process, prone to much anxiety, those words bring grace indeed. It is good to know that all *shall* be well. Here is no sunny optimism but a deep assurance of the ultimate victory of love. She captured what Paul meant when he told the Roman Christians experiencing "trouble, hardship, persecution, famine, nakedness, danger and the sword" that we *are* more than conquerors through him who loved us.

In her memorable words, Julian assures us, "He did not say, 'You shall not be tempest-tossed, you shall not be work-weary, you shall not be discomforted.' But he said, 'You shall not be overcome.'" I scribbled those words on a card and looked at them often during my days of recovery. Somehow they spoke to the deepest need of my soul. They were especially relevant because she had spoken them in the throes of acute sickness which almost took her life. Somehow they became a word from God for me, as I recalled the times when sickness *almost* overcame me, but did not. I shall continue to read Julian of Norwich as a new spiritual director!

LET US PRAY A PRAYER OF JULIAN:
God, of your goodness give me yourself
for you are sufficient for me.
I cannot properly ask anything less, to be worthy of you.
If I were to ask less, I should always be in want.
In you alone do I have all.
AMEN.

38

What I Learned from a Jigsaw Puzzle
READ 1 CORINTHIANS 12:12-20

*As it is, God has put all the separate parts into the body as he
chose. If they were all the same part, how could it be a body?
As it is, the parts are many but the body is one.*
(1 Corinthians 12:18-20, NJB)

ONE OF THE INGENIOUS WAYS MY WIFE helped me escape
boredom (and saved her own sanity) during the long
days and nights at home was buying me jigsaw
puzzles. I hadn't worked puzzles since childhood, when
we had no television to occupy our time and imprison
our minds. But I found this new pursuit to be a
fascinating time of discovery and discipline.

I learned that it took time to put the pieces
together, a gentle reminder that my recovery wouldn't
happen overnight. I also learned that there was real joy
in finding that missing piece, and every piece that
found its rightful place became part of the solution. It
made me realize that although there would be no
"quick fix" for my wounds, every small step each day
was a piece of the puzzle that would some day bring
the whole picture.

I remembered Paul's words to the Corinthians
about the unity of the church, likening it to the human
body. He says that a body works best when all
members contribute their part. Every member of the
body is essential, and even those parts of the body that
seem to be weaker are indispensable. Just as every piece

of the puzzle is essential, so every member of the body is valued and needed.

One of my friends, William Dugger, composed a song entitled "Different Pieces." Its opening verse goes like this:

If all the body were an eye . . .where then would be the hearing? / If all the body were an ear, where then would be the speaking? / Pieces . . . Diff'rent pieces . . . It takes all of them, / each one must fit in, then we can begin, / to solve the puzzle.

What is true for the unity of the church is equally true for healing. Different pieces are needed: the skill and dedication of the medical team; the patient care of nurses and family; the positive attitude of the sick person. Only when these pieces fit together can the puzzle of health begin to take shape.

Working jigsaw puzzles was great therapy. My greatest accomplishment was completing a 1,000 piece puzzle of Van Gogh's *Fishing Boats on the Beach at Saintes-Maries*. It still occupies a significant place in my study, a perpetual reminder of how different pieces bring wholeness.

GOD OF WHOLENESS,
We thank you for every person and experience
in the puzzle of our sickness.
We know we needed them to find the wholeness of health.
AMEN.

39

Christ's Prayer for the Sick
READ LUKE 22:31-34

*Simon, Simon! Look, Satan has got his wish to sift you all
like wheat; but I have prayed for you . . . that your faith may
not fail, and once you have recovered,
you in your turn must strengthen your brothers.*
(Luke 22:32, NJB)

WHAT AN UNFORGETTABLE MOMENT! Peter bragging
that Jesus could count on him when everyone else
failed, and Jesus gently reminding Peter that he *would*
fail. But Jesus' prayer was that Peter's faith would not
fail and when he had recovered he would strengthen
others. Jesus knew that Peter would fail, for weakness
was greater than his brash claims.

Peter's *faith* did not fail. His collapse was a new
beginning. In fact, his failure became the very door
through which he later experienced the grace of Christ.
In that post-resurrection experience, Jesus forgave Peter
and recommissioned him (John 21:15-19).

I often thought of Jesus' prayer when my patience
and courage failed during sickness. Jesus was praying
for *me*, that my faith not fail. Prayer is a vital force in
recovery from sickness. Stanley Hauerwas does not
decry the valuable skills of medical people in the
healing process. They are essential people on the road
back to health. He adds,

But no matter how powerful that craft becomes, it cannot in principle rule out the necessity of prayer. For prayer is not a supplement to the insufficiency of our medical knowledge and practice; nor is it some divine insurance policy that our medical skill will work; rather, our prayer is the means that we have to make God present whether our medical skill is successful or not.

Kathleen Fischer shows how prayer makes a difference to God.

It adds a new dimension to the situation . . . [Prayers] insert new love and strength into the situation of the person we are praying for, and they are received by God. . . . Prayer not only changes us; it affects God and those we pray for.

Jesus' prayer for Peter changed his life. His faith did not fail, and later he became the one who strengthened others in the faith.

I vividly recall a previous surgery at St. Joseph's Hospital in Asheville, North Carolina. Looking from my bed I saw the crucifix on the wall. Then and now it reminded me of the suffering Christ who prays for me.

PETER'S BENEDICTION
And the God of all grace, who called you to his eternal glory
in Christ, after you have suffered a little while,
will himself restore you
and make you strong, firm, and steadfast.
AMEN.
(1 Peter 5:10, NIV)

40

Songs at Midnight
READ ACTS 16:25-34

About midnight Paul and Silas
were praying and singing hymns to God . . .
(Acts 16:25a, NRSV)

ONE OF THE MOST DIFFICULT ASPECTS of being confined
at home is missing worship in the church. Whether as a
worship leader or a participant in the pew, worship was
always the peak moment of my week. Like the psalmist
I could exclaim, "I was glad when they said to me, 'Let
us go to the house of the Lord!' " (Psalm 122:1, NRSV).
For several weeks I had to stay at home and watch
church services by television. Although a real ministry
to the sick and shut-in, they cannot replace being
present in the house of the Lord.

On one particular Lord's Day, I wandered outside
and began pacing up and down in the restricted space
which was permitted me. Suddenly I began singing
hymns of faith. I knew most of them by heart and
thanked God that these songs of faith had been part of
my spiritual heritage. It became a moment of grace and
deliverance.

I remembered seeing a former student who
reminded me of one of my trivia questions from long-
ago Bible study. "Who sang hymns at midnight?" And I
relived Paul and Silas in the Philippian jail singing at
midnight. They were thrown into the inner prison,
some dungeon from which light was excluded and

probably all air was shut out. In that dungeon, in the darkness of night, their feet fast in stocks, their backs all bloody, they sang hymns of praise! Imprisoned in body, yet free in soul.

The earth shook, the prison was rattled, the doors flew open, and everyone's chains fell off. The jailer now was prisoner to his terror. Paul and Silas were free. Those who know suffering are the very ones who can sing.

One of the hymns I sang that morning was Henry F. Lyte's *Praise, My Soul, the King of Heaven.* The music and words linger.

> Praise, my soul, the King of heaven,
> To his feet thy tribute bring;
> Ransomed, healed, restored, forgiven,
> Evermore his praises sing.

I remembered a priceless story that my sister, Mary, who is a nurse, told me about a little boy dying of leukemia in a crowded hospital ward. It was Christmas Eve, and a mournful silence filled the ward. The frail little boy began to sing, "Jingle bells, jingle bells, jingle all the way," and soon other voices began to sing along with the dying child. Soon the whole hospital ward was bathed with the music of Christmas. So it is that Christ takes the pain of the whole world and makes it sing! Songs at midnight.

A MOMENT FOR MEDITATION
In a moment of quiet, whether in a hospital, at home, or any place, recall a favorite hymn and sing it.

41

Small Blessings for the Sickroom
READ JOHN 6:1-13

Who despises the day of small things?
(*Zechariah 4:10, NIV*)

WHILE I WAS RECUPERATING AT HOME, I received a precious card from two little children from a former parish with the following words (deciphered by their mother): "I love your joches *(jokes)*, and you prech *(preach)* good. You are one of the bestest fernd *(friend)* I ever had. I am sorry that you are herting *(hurting)*." — Alex and Jennifer

A small blessing for a bad time. That card from those little children really brightened my day, and I kept looking at it again and again.

It reminded me of the gift of the small boy when Jesus faced a hungry multitude. There was no way they could *buy* enough bread to feed that crowd. But Andrew singled out a boy with five barley loaves and two small fish. Perhaps Andrew knew the boy and had taken him fishing in his boat.

But that seemed so inadequate, and Andrew asked, "How far will they go among so many?" Jesus took the small gift of the boy and fed the multitudes. The significant thing is that although the boy's picnic lunch didn't look like much, little sandwich rolls and fish the size of sardines, Jesus used the child's gift to bless people.

Nothing means more during sickness than small acts of kindness, the "cup of cold water given in his name." In Dostoyevsky's novel *The Brothers Karamazov*, Dmitri has been sentenced to imprisonment in Siberia and is so exhausted that he falls asleep on a bench. When he awakens he finds that someone has placed a pillow under his head. A small act of kindness, but large in meaning.

Think of what it means when you are sick to have those small acts of kindness done for you. Someone who mows your yard, runs your errands as God's gopher, or brings meals from the church pantry. No wonder the ancient prophet asked, "Who despises the day of small things?" No one. It is the little, unnamed acts of kindness that you never forget.

Months later, I still look at Alex and Jennifer's card and their words of concern. It meant a lot that they took time to remember me. A small blessing but a lasting effect!

ETERNAL PARENT,
As our Parent, you understand our childish needs,
and we do need attention and love when we are sick.
Thank you for sending children to cheer us up.
AMEN.

42

Travels of the Mind
READ PHILIPPIANS 4:10-13

For as he thinks in his heart, so is he.
(Proverbs 23:7, NKJV)

ONE OF THE HARDEST THINGS FOR AN ACTIVE person to cope with when recovering from surgery is inactivity. As a person who has always needed to "be on the move," I found it incredibly hard to sit at home and view life from a window.

One source of help came from reading books. My brother, John, sent me a book by William Least Heat-Moon, *Blue Highways: A Journey into America*. On the title page he wrote these words, "One of my favorite, all-time books of wisdom. If you cannot travel physically, this will take you nonetheless. Recuperate. John"

I read this tale of an incredible 13,000-mile journey across America by a Native American, Least Heat-Moon, in his van he called "Ghost Dance." I traveled with him down back roads and through small, often forgotten towns, and recaptured the American experience.

I could not physically travel anywhere; indeed, for six weeks I could not go ten miles beyond my home. But through this book I have traveled down those blue highways, "when the open road is a beckoning, a strangeness, a place where a man can lose himself."

One sentence seemed written for me: "You never feel better than when you start feeling good after you've been feeling bad." That spoke to my condition as I grasped at the hope of feeling the renewed sense of energy that comes after recovery from surgery.

I remembered how Paul spent years in prison cells in Caesarea and Rome, and what restrictions those imprisonments placed on his tireless journeys for Christ. Yet from one prison cell he could write, "I have learned the secret of being content in any and every situation" (Phil. 4:12b, NIV). No doubt his mind wandered back to his missionary journeys as he sent letters to the young churches which he had established.

Two men occupied beds in a nursing home. The man by the door was completely paralyzed. The man by the window was very sick, but he remained alert and cheerful. The immobilized man asked his roommate to tell him what was happening out there in the world. So his friend described in vivid details many scenes from life outside the window: the mailman making his daily rounds; the social worker taking residents for a trip; the residents sitting quietly on lonely benches. One day the talkative man by the window died. Another man was wheeled into the room to take his place. The man next to the door asked his new roommate if he would be so kind as to tell him about the goings-on outside. "Sure," he replied, "only I don't know how I can. There's nothing outside *this* window but a solid brick wall."

ETERNAL KEEPER,
Teach us to find new ways to cope with restrictions.
AMEN.

43

Non-Anxious Family Standing By
READ JOHN 20:19-23

On the evening of that first day of the week,
when the disciples were together,
with the doors locked for fear of the Jews,
Jesus came and stood among them and said,
"Peace be with you!"
(John 20:19, NIV)

IT IS DIFFICULT TO BE A FAMILY MEMBER of a sick person.
When a person returns from the hospital, where care is
provided around the clock, he or she expects such care
to continue at home. Family members are busy people
coping with their own schedules, and now they must
take on the care of the sick person.

Alastair Campbell describes the difficult task of the
caregiver in this way:

Anyone who has entered into the darkness of
another's pain, loss, or bewilderment, and who has
done so without the defenses of a detached
professionalism, will know the feeling of wanting to
escape, of wishing they had not become involved.
Caring is costly, unsettling, even distasteful at times.
The valley of deep shadows in another person's life
frightens us too, and we lack the courage and
constancy to enter it.

Nothing means more in spiritual support for a sick person than family members who provide ongoing care.

When the disciples sat behind locked doors for fear of the Jews on that first explosive Easter Day, Jesus suddenly appeared and quietly said, "Peace be with you!" His non-anxious presence must have calmed the anxious hearts of the disciples and healed their hurt.

We do need caregivers whose non-anxious presence reassures us. Caring does not mean curing. As Henri Nouwen points out,

> To care is to cry out with those who are ill . . . and to recognize their pains in our own heart. . . . To care is to be present to those who suffer and to stay present even when nothing can be done to change their situation.

I was fortunate in having a wife whose care and non-anxious presence guided me over many difficult roads. She was always present, speaking the right word of comfort or confrontation and allowing me the freedom to express my fears. My extended family's help was limited to long-distance telephone calls, but their reassurance and concern brought genuine comfort.

A sick person at home does disrupt the whole family system. The sooner the sick person can participate in his or her care, the better for everyone. But the long gray days of sickness can be brightened by a supportive family.

GOD WHO HAS SET THE SOLITARY IN FAMILIES,
We pause to thank you for our families, who stand with us in sickness. As they have prayed for us, we now pray with gratitude for them.
AMEN.

V

Crawling to the Gate Called Beautiful

The human body experiences a powerful gravitational pull

in the direction of hope.

That is why the patient's hopes are the

physician's secret weapon.

They are the hidden ingredients in any prescription.

NORMAN COUSINS

44

Creep Before You Leap
READ ACTS 3:1-10

Now a man crippled from birth was being carried
to the temple gate called Beautiful. . . . He jumped to his feet
and began to walk. Then he went with them into the temple
courts, walking and jumping, and praising God.
(Acts 3:2a,8, NIV)

ONE YEAR WE PLANTED IVY around some trees in our yard. The owner of the garden center advised us, "Remember this about ivy: the first year it sleeps; the second year it creeps; and the third year it leaps." When ivy is watered and cared for, it will sleep, creep, and leap.

The crippled man at the gate called Beautiful in the temple did what every dependent and helpless person often does—he asked for a handout. He had no other hope than to live by the crumbs he could beg from others. To the man's surprise, he received more than he asked for. He asked for alms; he received healing.

Peter did not give him "silver and gold" but told him "in the name of Jesus Christ of Nazareth, walk" (Acts 3:6). And the man, lame from birth, jumped to his feet and began to walk. The man who had crawled or been carried by others leapt to his feet, walked and jumped, and praised God.

I have learned that recovery from sickness does take time. The rules for growth in the spiritual sense are different from the rules for growth in the physical world. Disease and disaster can wipe out prosperity.

But spiritual growth *depends* on adversity. As ivy sleeps and creeps before it leaps, growth in the spiritual world takes times and involves pain.

The noted author Max Lerner suffered life-threatening illnesses that began when he was seventy-eight, with two successive cancers and a heart attack. In his deeply moving narrative *Wrestling with the Angel* he talks about his struggle:

> Every patient, as Albert Schweitzer saw, carries a doctor, as healer, within himself. Everything connected with illness is a wounding experience. It is an inspiring thing to think of both patient and "doctor within the patient" as part of the healing process, and to see both as using the healing to recover from their wounds.

Illness evokes a creative force! But we must creep before we can leap. Like that lame man at the gate called Beautiful, symbolic of healing, I had to crawl before I could walk. But those difficult days released the "doctor within me," and eventually brought healing.

STRENGTHENING GOD,
At times when we are sick, we chafe and resist
the long days and weeks of getting well.
Help us to believe that these times are releasing the
"doctor within us," so that we can at last walk.
AMEN.

45

Facing Health's Enemies
READ PSALM 27

Though an army besiege me,
my heart will not fear.
(Psalm 27:3a, NIV)

MY FIRST PASTORATE WAS AT THE Presbyterian church of Moorefield, West Virginia. During the Civil War, the town felt the force of the fighting. Because it was close to the border, one day it would be controlled by Union troops, the next day by the Confederates.

In the center of town, an old woman lived alone. According to the report of a Presbyterian minister, one morning enemy soldiers knocked at her door and demanded breakfast. She asked them in and said she would prepare some food for them. When the food was ready, she said, "It is my custom to read the Bible and pray before breakfast. I hope you won't mind." They consented, so she opened her Bible and began to read, "The Lord is my light and my salvation; whom shall I fear? The Lord is the strength of my life; of whom shall I be afraid?" She finished the psalm and said, "Let us pray." While praying, she heard sounds of the soldiers in the room. She looked up. The soldiers were gone!

Sickness brings many enemies to harass us, not the least of which is anxiety. We get anxious about our recovery—why does it take so long, and will we ever feel better again? We worry about missing work or being a burden to our families. And this anxiety depletes our strength and impedes our progress.

We *do* need to be concerned. Recovering from sickness is not as simple as, "Have faith. Take three Bible verses and you will be well." Our biggest enemy in getting well is the strangling anxiety which can immobilize us. I remember a little verse from childhood,

The worry cow would have lasted until now
If she only saved her breath.
But she thought her hay wouldn't last all day,
So she mooed herself to death.

We need the faith of the Moorefield woman when she faced her enemies. Psalm 27 affirms that "in the day of trouble he will keep me safe in his dwelling" (Psalm 27:5, NIV). So the psalmist urges us to "wait for the LORD; be strong and take heart and wait for the LORD" (Psalm 27:14, NIV).

Jesus promised us peace from this major enemy: "In me you may have peace. In this world you will have trouble" (John 16:33*a*, NIV). His peace does not consist in having no enemies. It is freedom from anxiety while struggling *with* enemies, in spite of the threat. The one who has learned the secret of true peace is the one who is at peace even when there are many reasons not to be.

O BLESSED AND GRACIOUS GOD,
Who only canst heal a wounded spirit
and quiet a troubled mind; unto thee do I cry for help.
O thou great Physician of body and soul,
uphold and comfort my weak and dejected spirit. . . .
Oh, hear my most earnest supplication
and make me to possess an easy, quiet, and cheerful spirit,
as my trust is in thee.
AMEN.
(Prayer of John Wesley)

God's Convalescent Clothes
READ COLOSSIANS 3:12-17

*And the LORD God made garments of skin for the
man and for his wife, and clothed them.
(Genesis 3:21, NRSV)*

ONE SIGN OF MY RECOVERY WAS THE RED-LETTER day
when I could shed my "sick clothes" and put on real
clothes again. I knew then that my invalid days were
ending, and health was returning. Being sick is a naked
experience. Despite the efforts of caring people, there
are humiliating experiences which leave you
vulnerable. Your wounds become all too visible and, as
Adam and Eve discovered, there is no place to hide.

God mercifully gave our spiritual parents new
clothes to cover their nakedness after the Fall. Only then
could they face the world and look at each other.
Clothed by the Creator's grace, they could make their
way in a world marred by their sin.

Frederick Buechner says of this moment,

> They can't go back, but they can go forward clothed
> in a new way—clothed, that is, not in the sense of
> having their old defenses again behind which to hide
> who they are and what they have done but in the
> sense of having a new understanding of who they are
> and a new strength to draw on for what lies before
> them to do now.

Paul urged the Christians at Colossae to put on new clothes. When a Christian was baptized, he or she took off the old clothes and put on new, white robes. Paul urged them, "Clothe yourselves with compassion, kindness, humility, meekness, and patience. . . . Above all, clothe yourselves with love" (Col. 3:12b, 14a, NRSV). As Christians, these do become our new clothes in our new life with Christ.

God graciously gives sick persons "new clothes" as we stumble to recovery and discover new strength to draw on for what lies ahead.

God clothes the nakedness of our fretfulness with patience.

God clothes the nakedness of our despair with hope.

God clothes the nakedness of our irritability with compassion.

God clothes the nakedness of our sins with love.

Yes, it was a good day when I took off the pajamas and put on my clothes. I wore a sweatshirt that first day that placarded the words *CARPE DIEM*, "Seize the Day." But on a deeper level, God has clothed us with gifts of grace and love which means we never again have to hide behind our old defenses. We can be who we are. We can openly share our wounds. We can be vulnerable in our relationships. Now we can be secure in the new strength and grace which only God can give.

MERCIFUL GOD,
We praise you for being so merciful
when our sickness makes us want to hide from others.
May your incredible love be our new clothes.
AMEN.

Autumn Thoughts
READ PSALM 92

They will still bear fruit in old age,
they will stay fresh and green.
(Psalm 92:14, NIV)

IN THE EARLY DAYS OF RECOVERING FROM surgery I was able to take short walks in the neighborhood. One late October day I walked aimlessly in the waning moments of autumn. My attention focused on a beautiful maple tree, and I marveled at its mixture of bright gold and blazing red. That tree became a favorite sight on my recovery walks.

Later I noticed that a harsh wind had stripped every leaf from that tree, and it stood empty and barren, its golden glory only a memory. A wistful sadness filled my heart, and I knew why. Falling leaves of autumn remind us of death. Joyce Rupp says,

> The leaves are subtle reminders that we are asked to let go of many things throughout our life. Every time we must surrender something, we connect with our death, with the ultimate moment of letting go.

Yet, I took heart as I remembered that the tree stood strong and firm, despite the loss of its leaves. I remembered Mary Fahy's beautiful book *The Tree that Survived the Winter* and saw a parable of my own recovery. Like that tree, I was beginning to "embrace more of the world . . . with the freedom of knowing that the wind could not topple [me]." I, too, had been stripped of strength and physical stamina. I knew I would never be the same. The aging process does bring inevitable losses, and surgery compounds those losses.

I thought of Psalm 92: "The righteous will flourish like a palm tree . . . [they] will still bear fruit in old age, they will stay fresh and green" (Psalm 92:12a, 14, NIV). The sadness of the fallen leaves is transformed by the realization that barren branches already bear potential of new green in their buds.

The autumn days are followed by winter snows while the earth waits in the process of growth for the coming of another spring. Yes, autumn does remind us of letting go and of death, but it is also a harbinger of another spring when life begins again.

Perhaps we are more preoccupied with the *body* beautiful than the *person* beautiful. Some of my resiliency and strength is gone. But, like the tree that survived the winter, I am growing as I await a new springtime of the soul.

GOD OF THE SEASONS,
We thank you for the autumn of the year,
a time of harvest and hopes.
Grant that we may let go of that which clings too closely
in order that new life can spring forth.
AMEN.

48

Ordinary Saints
READ PHILIPPIANS 2:12-13

Enter through the narrow gate . . .
small is the gate and narrow the road
that leads to life, and only a few find it.
(Matthew 7:13a-14, NIV)

ONE OF THE BOOKS THAT DEEPLY INFLUENCED ME during the long days and nights of my recovery was Marsha Sinetar's *Ordinary People as Monks and Mystics*. She makes the bold claim: "Ordinary, everyday people can and do become whole.... People who become whole are the ones who find completeness by consciously integrating inner and outer realities." Based on interviews with ordinary people who live solitary, reflective lives, her book points the way to sainthood.

Years ago I was influenced by Albert Edward Day's book *Discipline and Discovery*. First published in 1947, this book encouraged me to *try* to live the Christian life. Day said,

We have loudly proclaimed our dependence upon the grace of God, never guessing that the *grace* of God is given only to those who practice the *grace of self–mastery*. "Work out your own salvation with fear and trembling for God is at work in you both to will and to work his good pleasure." Persons working out, God working in—that is the New Testament synthesis.

Notice that Paul did not say, "Work *for* your salvation." We are to work *out* our salvation as God works *in* us. For years I had to practice these disciplines of the inner life, always falling far short. However, during the enforced spaces of silence that sickness brought me, I found myself working again on the disciplines of obedience, simplicity, humility, frugality, generosity, truthfulness, purity, and charity. Ordinary people *can* become mystics if we are willing to pay the price.

The cruise control in automobiles is a fascinating device. Once the automobile is headed toward its destination and the desired speed is achieved, the cruise control can be activated, allowing the driver to sit back and relax his or her leg and foot. Not so with the Christian life. We cannot simply turn our lives over to God, switch to cruise control and coast into the heavenly city. Jesus' words are all too clear: "Small is the gate and narrow the road that leads to life, and only a few find it."

Yet I learned in those difficult days of weakness that this life with God *is* a possibility. Sinetar concludes,

If we want this type of perfection—namely completion as a personality—then we must give ourselves the time in which to grow, for this will not happen overnight. . . . We will need to design our lives so that there is quiet, reflective time to become what we know we already are at some deeper level.

Yes, it takes a lifetime and more for ordinary people to become saints!

GOD WHO CALLS US TO BECOME SAINTS,
When we are sick, help us to use this time of
enforced quiet as an opportunity for growth.
AMEN.

49

Meditations from a Sickbed
READ ROMANS 14:1-8

*We do not live to ourselves, and we do not die
to ourselves. If we live, we live to the Lord,
and if we die, we die to the Lord; so, then,
whether we live or whether we die, we are the Lord's.*
(Romans 14:7-8, NRSV)

ONE OF MY FRIENDS, A MINISTER, SUGGESTED that I read John Donne's *Devotions* during my long weeks of confinement. Donne wrote these devotions in the throes of great pain, when he was convinced he was dying. His wife had died of the bubonic plague, and a few years later he was diagnosed with the same disease. The illness dragged on, sapping his strength.

In *Devotions*, Donne expressed anger at God. It seemed unfair that just at the moment he had begun his first work as a parish minister, he was stricken with this deadly illness. He found no meaning in this misfortune until he heard church bells from his bedroom window tolling their mournful news of death.

At first he thought that his own death was imminent and that his friends had ordered the bells rung for his demise. But quickly he realized the bells signaled a neighbor's death from the plague.

Donne wrote Meditation XVII on the meaning of the church bells. It is one of the most celebrated passages in English literature.

No man is an island, entire of itself; every man is a piece of the continent, a part of the main. . . . any man's death diminishes me, because I am involved in mankind, and therefore never send to know for whom the bell tolls; it tolls for thee.

Donne realized that although the bells had been sounded in honor of another's death, they served a stark reminder that we all will die. Donne realized that his life, even in his bedridden state, was not meaningless. So he focused on spiritual disciplines: prayer, keeping a journal, and concern for others. Donne's prayer was no longer that his pain be removed but that it be redeemed. Psalm 41:3 was an important verse for him: "The LORD sustains them on their sickbed; in their illness you heal all their infirmities" (NRSV).

When you are sick, you do hear the bell tolling, and life becomes more precious as death becomes more real.

Theologian Joseph Sittler wrote,

The fear of death, I'm convinced, is at the bottom of all apprehensions. To say of any of us that we do not fear death is a lie. To be human is to fear death. . . . And all people fear death. . . . But what life beyond death might be, I have no notion. Something continues, but what that will be I'm perfectly willing to leave in the hands of the Originator.

LOVING GOD,
Help us so to live each day
that death will be just another chapter of our journey.
AMEN.

50

The Hormah Syndrome
READ NUMBERS 14:36-45

*But they presumed to go up to the heights of the hill country
. . . Then the Amalekites and the Canaanites . . . came down
and defeated them, pursuing them as far as Hormah.*
(Numbers 14:44a-45, NRSV)

THE ISRAELITES WERE WARNED BY MOSES not to invade
Canaan. Their refusal to believe the minority report of
Joshua and Caleb betrayed their lack of faith. They
refused to obey Moses' words, and in a rash moment
attacked their enemies and were defeated and driven to
Hormah. It took forty years of discipline in the desert
before they could occupy the land.

I learned the hard lesson while recovering from
surgery that we may rush things too quickly. I was
warned not to overdo, but when that old energy
returned, I took a short trip into town and paid the
price. My Hormah became a delay in recovery and
longer discipline of rest and passivity.

The Israelites tried to do in remorse what they
failed to do in faith. They thought they could rush in
and claim the land in *their* time. But God knew they
were not ready. Their terror at the words that giants
were in the land proved they would have been easy
prey for their enemies, so God had other plans. And
they included delay and discipline.

It is easy to throw caution to the wind and plunge
into activities too soon. We want to resume our routine,
recapture life the way it was, without realizing it never

will be the same. The question Paul asked the Galatians comes to us, "You were running a good race. Who cut in on you and kept you from obeying the truth?" (Gal. 5:7, NIV) Usually it is our own impatience and impulsiveness.

We need to learn to take a day at a time, not feel guilty for inactivity, and let the healing powers take their time. One of the hymns that I often thought about after this setback was, "Because I Knew Not When My Life Was Good." One of the verses spoke to me:

Because I was impatient, would not wait,
And thrust my willful hand across Thy threads,
And marred the pattern drawn out for my life,
O Lord, I do repent.

I am sure the Israelites repented after their stunning defeat at Hormah. They knew they had to face the rigors of the wilderness before they could claim their promised land. I knew, too, that my momentary relapse taught me a hard lesson, that I needed to be patient and go through some more discomfort before I could claim the promise of healing. Hormah is a momentary setback, but not the whole picture!

GOD OF COMFORT,
*We confess that we try to force things and speed up
our recovery, only to prolong it by our foolishness.
But you understand,
and discipline us for our own good.*
AMEN.

51

When There's Hope, There's Life
READ ROMANS 5:1-4, 8:18-25

*May the God of hope fill you with all joy and peace
in believing, so that you may abound in hope
by the power of the Holy Spirit.
(Romans 15:13, NRSV)*

ALL OF US HAVE HEARD THE OLD SAYING, "Where there's life, there's hope." Perhaps you have quoted it in times of crisis or illness. The reverse is also true for sick persons. "Where there's hope, there's life." Norman Cousins, in his book *Head First: The Biology of Hope,* expressed this need when he wrote,

> Illness is a terrifying experience. Something is happening that people don't know how to deal with. They are reaching out not just for medical help but for ways of thinking about catastrophic illness. *They are reaching out for hope. (Italics mine)*

Many times during my illness I hoped for better days. Once I penned these words in my journal:

> "Some day"—that is the constant hope of every sick person. Some day life will return to some semblance of normalcy. Some day things will be different, and my pain gone. Some day I will not have to live under this dark cloud. Some day. Until then I must have faith and take courage. I do not know why I have had such a hard time with this surgery, while other men

seem to breeze through it. I must *live* those classic words, *"Be patient in tribulation."*

Paul often wrote about hope. In his letter to the Romans he said, "But if we hope for what we do not yet have, we wait for it patiently" (Rom. 8:25, NIV). He believed the created world waited with eager expectation for the day when God's glory would be revealed. His words describe the attitude of a person who scans the horizon eagerly searching for the first signs of the dawn of glory.

So, we can "exult in our troubles," since these adverse forces serve the ultimate "hope," being made into the likeness of God. So, Paul writes, "We also boast in our sufferings, knowing that suffering produces endurance, and endurance produces character, and character produces hope, and hope does not disappoint us, because God's love has been poured into our hearts through the Holy Spirit that has been given to us" (Rom. 5:3-5, NRSV).

There *is* hope. Hope is the ability to imagine life in another way. Life with health restored; or life beyond with perfect joy and peace. With Isaac Watts we can affirm,

> O God, our help in ages past
> Our hope for years to come,
> Be thou our guide while life shall last,
> And our eternal home.

O GOD OF HOPE,
Let those words fill our lives with
joy and peace in believing.
AMEN.

52

Only If You've Been There
READ HEBREWS 4:14–5:10

I sat where they sat,
and remained there astonished
among them for seven days.
(Ezekiel 3:15, NKJV)

EZEKIEL WAS NOT EXACTLY IN A GOOD FRAME of mind to give pastoral care to the exiles at Tel-abib. He went to them by the River Chebar "in bitterness, in the heat of my spirit." He had little sympathy for those exiles, and no real heart for serving them. He must have asked himself the questions, "Why do they act the way they do? What *is* their problem? What is really going on inside their skin?"

He sat where they sat by the River Chebar for seven days, and his bitterness dissolved and his attitude changed. He listened to them, really understood their plight, and finally identified himself with them. In Camus's novel *The Plague*, Father Paneloux at first tries to reconcile the plague with God's justice and mercy. But when he sees an innocent child die, something seems to change in him. He has no easy answers, only a deeper compassion for those who suffered.

Only as Ezekiel shared the people's plight did he begin to realize what it was like to be an exile in a captivity which had gone on for far too long. I have discovered that the people who can *really* understand what it is like to be sick are those who have been there.

We have a good example in our Lord, who consistently identified with the sick, the poor, and the outcasts. His compassionate ministry was summarized in the words of the prophet, "Yet ours were the sufferings he was bearing, ours the sorrows he was carrying" (Isa. 53:4, NJB). So the writer to the Hebrews could say of him, "We do not have a High Priest who cannot sympathize with our weaknesses, but he was in all points tempted as we are, yet without sin" (Heb. 4:15, NKJV).

Henri Nouwen points us to an old legend in the *Talmud* in which Rabbi Yoshua ben Levi asks the prophet Elijah, "When will the Messiah come?" Elijah replies that the Messiah will be "sitting at the gates of the city. . . . sitting among the poor covered with wounds." Jesus sat with us with untiring patience and died crucified between two thieves, not between two candles.

When we experience the healing that comes from others who have "been there" and can touch us with genuine empathy, then we can reach out as healed victims to help others.

———

GOD WHO SITS WITH US,
We would follow your example
and sit with those who suffer, being attentive to them,
neither shutting off their true feelings by our hasty solutions
nor leaving them because we cannot stand the discomfort.
AMEN.

53

Parable Walks
READ LUKE 24:13-35

*Do two walk together
unless they have agreed to do so?
(Amos 3:3, NIV)*

TWO PEOPLE WALK FROM JERUSALEM TO Emmaus with heavy hearts. Recent events in Jerusalem have destroyed their dreams. They come upon a stranger who seems to know nothing of the tragic death of their messiah. They share their story of disillusionment, and the stranger interprets the story, making their scripture come alive with meaning. In the village of Emmaus this stranger becomes known to them as their Lord, and they rush back to Jerusalem to tell the story of hopes lost and now found.

Flora Slosson Wuellner, in her delightful book *Prayer and Our Bodies*, talks about *parable walks*. "Try taking a 'parable walk,' in which you set out with no special agenda, asking God to show you something that will be meaningful, relevant to your problems and feelings."

She goes on to say that what you experience may not be anything sensational. In fact, it may be something as simple as "the way a tree is shaped, what an ant is doing, or how a bird is sounding. . . . someone's face, the way the breeze feels, or the way a dog is barking."

During my long time of confinement at home, parable walks were an important part of my healing. It was amazing what God showed me. At first it was some of my neighbors whom I had never really met. At other times it was the wonderful world of nature . . . the sound of birds, the golden beauty of autumn, the warm sunshine on my face.

I remember seeing a yellow cat sauntering up a driveway with such an unperturbed pace that she reminded me to "take it easy." One of my favorite friends on these walks was a neighbor's beautiful collie named Buck. How many delightful conversations we had over the fence!

It is a tragedy that we have become such a sedentary people. Walking energizes our spirits, clears out the cobwebs, and is great therapy. God speaks to us not only in ordinary things but also in gentle nudges that come as we walk. I believe walking is a kind of prayer as we slow down and listen for the "still, small voice."

Cleopas and the unnamed other found the living Lord on their Emmaus walk. When the stranger from Nazareth left them, they asked each other, "Were not our hearts burning within us as he talked to us on the road, while he opened to us the scriptures?" I've often wondered, *What if they had not taken that walk on Easter afternoon? They would have missed the risen Lord!*

LIVING LORD,
*Bless us with new insight as we walk with you,
and bring to those of us who cannot walk
some other means of grace.*
AMEN.

54

If You Can Take It, You Can Make It
READ 2 CORINTHIANS 12:1-9

*Wherefore, so that I should not get above myself,
I was given a thorn in the flesh.*
(2 Corinthians 12:7, NJB)

PAUL HAD SOME REAL PROBLEM THAT PLAGUED his life.
He called it a "thorn in the flesh," and whatever it was,
he was stuck with it for life. Scholars have debated what
this "thorn" was. Some have argued that it was opposi-
tion from people. Although people can be a pain at
times, it seems more likely that it was a chronic illness
that would not go away.

William Sloane Coffin says that it could have been
a "psychosomatic problem," or even a purely psycho-
logical disorder. He argues that for us a "thorn" can be
a divorce, or a child who has disgraced us, or some
stupid mistake we have made. Whatever Paul's thorn
was, and whatever the thorn for each of us is, Coffin
says, "Thorns are what we are stuck with."

Paul learned that "his strength was made perfect in
weakness," so he found grace to take this thorn in
stride. Marianne Williamson aptly describes how sickness can be a "wake-up call."

Many people have spoken of their illnesses as a
"wake-up call." That means wake up and experience
life—wake up and bless each morning, wake up and
appreciate friends and family. I have heard people
with critical illnesses say that their lives only really

began when they were diagnosed. Why is that? Because whenever we are diagnosed with a critical illness, much of our superficial personal baggage is dropped in the first five minutes.

Physician Larry Dossey tells of one of his patients who was dying from lung cancer. The day before his death the patient sat with his wife and children. The man knew he had little time left and chose his words carefully, speaking in a hoarse whisper. Although not a religious person, he revealed that recently he had begun to pray frequently. Dossey records the dialogue:

"What do you pray for?" I asked.
"I don't pray for anything," he responded. "How would I know what to ask for?" . . .
"If prayer is not for asking, what is it for?*" I pushed him.*
"It isn't 'for' anything," he said thoughtfully. "It mainly reminds me I am not alone."

At first Paul prayed for release from the thorn. Later he realized that God's grace was sufficient. *If we can take it, we can make it.* Sickness forces us to rearrange our priorities and wake up to life.

LORD,
Give me patience in tribulation
and grace in everything to conform my will to you,
that I may truly say: "Your will be done,
on earth as it is in heaven."
"The things, good Lord, that I pray for,
give me your grace to labor for."
AMEN.
(Sir Thomas More)

55

This, Too, Shall Pass
READ 2 CORINTHIANS 4:13-18

You shall surely forget your trouble,
recalling it only as waters gone by.
(Job 11:16, NIV)

LONG AGO, AN EASTERN MONARCH PLAGUED by many worries, harassed on every side, called his wise men together. He asked them to invent a motto, a few magic words that would help him in time of trial or distress. It must be brief enough to be engraved on a ring, he said, so that he could keep it always in his sight. It must be appropriate for any situation, good or bad. It had to be a motto by which persons could guide their lives in any circumstance, no matter what happened.

The wise men pondered this for a long time and finally came to the monarch with the magic words. They were words that would fit any situation, good or bad, words to ease the heart in every circumstance. The words they gave the monarch to be engraved on his ring were:

This, too, shall pass away.

How true for any situation! These words remind us that happy times come and go, and often seem better in anticipation than in realization. And difficult times also leave us. How often during the most difficult days of discomfort and pain did I ponder those words.

The apostle Paul captured this truth in a far deeper sense when he wrote to the Corinthians. He wrote, "For this slight momentary affliction is preparing us for an eternal weight of glory beyond all measure" (2 Cor. 4:17, NRSV). Present troubles are slight and momentary when viewed in the light of eternity. So Paul could proclaim, "I consider that the sufferings of this present time are not worth comparing with the glory about to be revealed to us" (Rom. 8:18, NRSV).

This, too, shall pass. On a difficult day when everything seemed to be going haywire, I thought about these words. That day I wrote this prayer:

UNDERSTANDING GOD,
I am discouraged and tired today,
But I'm not giving up.
I'm frazzled and frustrated today,
But life still goes on.

I'm anxious and a pest to people,
But I know they love me.
It's been a bad day today,
But it's only a day.

It will pass.
Give me patience to wait it out
And surrender my despair until another day.
AMEN.

If you are having a bad day, make this your prayer. If not, pray this for someone else!

56

Learning How to Rest
READ MARK 1:32-39

*Come with me by yourselves to a
quiet place and get some rest.*
(Mark 6:31, NIV)

MANY TIMES I HAVE READ THOSE WORDS in the first
chapter of Mark and glossed over them in my haste to
get on with the next dramatic piece of action in Jesus'
ministry. But Mark tell us, "In the morning, long before
dawn, [Jesus] got up and left the house and went off to
a lonely place and prayed there."

Picture the moment. Everything is dark, with no
sign yet of the light of day. A crowd of desperate people
sleep outside the house, waiting to be first in line for
healing by the Rabbi from Nazareth on the next day.
Only Jesus is awake at this early hour, and he slips out
of the house under cover of darkness. He goes to a
lonely place and prays.

What is significant is that he walked away from it
all. He well knew the needs of the crippled and sick
who waited for their chance at healing. But Jesus
needed to get away to rest . . . and pray. The disciples
searched for him until they found him and cried,
"Everyone is looking for you." They all wanted a piece
of him, but he needed to be alone and replenish his
soul.

People who experience sickness will soon discover
two truths: First, when energy begins to return, we
become restless and anxious about being inactive. And

second, we *do* need the rest that the days of recuperation grant us. Everyone feels the need at some time to escape from the pressures of life. We do need to rest, and one of the hidden blessings of sickness is that God gives us this respite from life's stress and strain.

The writer of the Twenty-third Psalm saw this truth when he wrote, "He makes me lie down in green pastures." There are times in life's journey when we must slow down and find some "away" space to be restored in soul.

Jesus went off to pray but after solitude and rest he went back to face the world and resume his healing ministry. We will find sickness a "lonely place" for prayer. We will get anxious when we find our strength not restored, our wounds still unhealed. But this time can be a moment of rest and renewal.

The great Japanese Christian pastor Toyohiko Kagawa was forced into a long inactivity due to illness. Hindered from carrying on his incredible social ministry in the depression Japan experienced in the 1930s, he was not restless, but said, "Work is not the purpose of my life. I am giving life that I may live. . . . My present task here and now is to be in fellowship with God." We need that kind of rest to be whole again.

GOD OF REST,
Grant that we find such rest in you,
such peace in your presence,
that nothing can disturb us.
AMEN.

VI

The Valley of Achor
Becomes a Door of Hope

Suffering can be beneficial when it leads to

some kind of "resurrection" in us,

when a strength or a sleeping energy in us is aroused,

when talents heretofore unknown are recognized,

when a clarity about life's purpose and direction

becomes keener for us,

when a stronger sense of compassion

for others deepens in us.

JOYCE RUPP

57

Troubles and Hope Go Together
READ HOSEA 2:14-25

There I will give her back her vineyards,
and will make the Valley of Achor a door of hope.
(Hosea 2:15, NIV)

THE LATE KENNETH J. FOREMAN TELLS about recalling a little series of pictures in the *New Yorker* showing an interesting event at a small bridge. Approaching the bridge, plainly marked LOAD LIMIT EIGHT TONS, was a truck, also marked on its side, EIGHT TONS. When the truck reached the middle of the bridge, a bluebird alighted on it. At that point the bridge gave way and crashed into the river, carrying the truck with it. The bridge could hold up under its load limit, but not under eight tons plus one bluebird.

Of course the story is fictional, but any bridge in the world has its breaking point. Anyway, it isn't the bluebird that causes the breakdown, but the eight tons already there. Troubles come to everyone, and sometimes we do break down under the pressure, especially when our load exceeds our limit.

The prophet Hosea finds that troubles and hope go together. Speaking for God, he says, "I will make the Valley of Achor a door of hope." The Valley of Achor (trouble) formed a portion of the northwest boundary of Judah, and marked the place where Achan had been stoned to death for his disobedience (Josh. 7:26). Hosea claims that this valley of trouble, which reminded the

Israelites of God's terrible judgment, would become a door of hope.

It is strange for trouble and hope to be placed in close proximity, especially in sickness. We usually say, "In spite of the trouble, we are hoping for the best" when confronted with sickness or other troubles. Hosea claims that the two are interrelated, that trouble leads to hope.

Through his own troubles with a wayward, adulterous wife, Gomer, Hosea found an open door to the unconditional love of God. Even as he could not give up loving troublesome Gomer, so Yahweh could not give up loving troublesome Israel. Our troubles can become doors of hope.

When we are troubled by sickness or other problems, we need to remember that God has no load limit and that God's love and grace are always available. The words of Frederick W. Faber's hymn ring true!

> There's a wideness in God's mercy,
> Like the wideness of the sea;
> There's a kindness in God's justice,
> Which is more than liberty.
> There is no place where earth's sorrows
> Are more felt than up in heaven;
> There is no place where earth's failings
> Have such kindly judgement given.

GOD OF HOPE,
Dare we believe that these troubles
can become doors of hope?
Help us so to believe as we cling
to your unconditional love.
AMEN.

58

Resurrection Medicine
READ PSALM 41

Yahweh sustains him on his bed of sickness;
you transform altogether the bed where he lies sick.
(Psalm 41:3, NJB)

IN HIS PROVOCATIVE BOOK, *Healing and the Mind*, Bill Moyers uses a phrase coined by Dr. Ron Anderson, "resurrection medicine." Anderson describes this phenomenon as "when patients come in literally at death's doorstep, and you're trying to pull them out of the jaws of death."

The writer of Psalm 41 experienced "resurrection medicine." He suffered from what appeared to be a "fatal sickness" (Psalm 41:8*a*), but God sustained him on his bed of sickness and rescued him from danger. So, the psalmist could exult, "in time of trouble Yahweh rescues him. Yahweh protects him, gives him life and happiness on earth" (Psalm 41:1*b*, 2, NJB).

Flora Slosson Wuellner talks about our trans-formed bodies, referring to life beyond death:

We will not experience any sense of fragmentation or separation between body and spirit then. We will experience a unity that is almost unimaginable to us now. The unity of God's light flashing and flowing without break from spirit to form and from form to spirit will have become the passionate oneness that was always God's will, God's longing for us.

But she goes on to claim that we do not need to wait for death to begin to experience the healing of this fragmentation between body and spirit. "Resurrected life can begin now!"

Whenever we experience a life-threatening illness and are spared, we know what it means to experience resurrected life. Stephen Levine says that healing involves "extra wellness," a healing "into life."

> Healing is what happens when we come to our edge, to the unexplored territory of mind and body, and take a single step beyond into the unknown, the space in which all growth occurs. Healing is discovery. It goes beyond life and death.

Henri Nouwen, writing about his near-lethal accident and resultant journey to that shadowland between life and death, says,

> My experience of God's love during my hours near death has given me a renewed knowledge of not belonging to the world—the dark powers of our society. . . . I am a child of God. . . . I am held safe in the intimacy of divine love.

So as we recover from serious illness, especially if we have come precariously close to the edge of the cliff, we find an "extra wellness." We experience "resurrection medicine" as a foretaste of what the gospel means, that God has healed us in life and death.

RESURRECTING GOD,
Let us completely trust the Risen Lord
so that we may completely belong to you and be free
to live fully in this world.
AMEN.

59

Hezekiah Discovered It
READ ISAIAH 38:1–39:8

Lord, by such things men live;
and my spirit finds life in them too.
You restored me to health and let me live.
(Isaiah 38:16,17a, NIV)

KING HEZEKIAH SUFFERED FROM SOME critical illness, the nature of which we do not know. But he was ill, "at the point of death." When Isaiah the prophet told the king to "put his house in order" because he would not recover, Hezekiah prayed for deliverance. God heard his prayer, healed his disease, and prolonged his life fifteen years.

Hezekiah wrote a psalm of praise after his illness and recovery. With an outburst of thanksgiving the king declared, "You restored me to health and let me live." Then he added, "Surely it was for my benefit that I suffered such anguish."

Anyone who has experienced critical illnesses or faced anxious moments after surgery can identify with Hezekiah's experience. There were times when we too wondered if we would be robbed of the rest of our years. Hezekiah discovered that it was Yahweh who restored him to health. For those with the eyes of faith, that is also our discovery.

Like Hezekiah, we discover the key to healing in the darkness. Anthony del Mello records this parable:

A neighbor found Nasrudin on hands and knees.
"What are you searching for, Mullah?"
"My key."
Both men got on their knees to search.
After a while the neighbor said, "Where did you lose it?"
"At home."
"Good Lord! Then why are you searching here?"
"Because it's brighter here."

Georg Neumark was a German poet and hymn writer of the seventeenth century. He had his share of hardships. He was robbed of his life's savings and had to postpone his education. He lost all of his household possessions in a fire, and later became blind. Yet his faith never wavered, and in 1657 he wrote this hymn:

> If thou but trust in God to guide thee,
> With hopeful heart through all thy ways,
> God will give strength, whate'er betide thee,
> To bear thee through the evil days.
> . . . .
> God never yet forsook at need
> The soul secured by trust indeed.

If you have known times when God has healed you or some loved one, take a moment to offer a prayer of thanksgiving.

———————

GRACIOUS GOD,
Others have helped me get well,
and I have tried to fight the good fight,
but you alone are the Healer.
Thank you for restoring me to health.
AMEN.

60

Beware of Asa's Doctors!
READ 2 CHRONICLES 16:11-14

*Asa contracted a disease in his feet,
which became very severe. In his illness,
however, he consulted not Yahweh,
but the doctors.*
(2 Chronicles 16:12, NJB)

HIDDEN IN THE BOOK OF CHRONICLES is a short word about sickness and doctors. King Asa suffered from a severe illness. He consulted doctors who were cast in a disparaging light by the chronicler. In those days making an appointment with a doctor instead of praying to God indicated a lack of faith. Apparently the doctors' medicine failed, for two years later the king died.

Beware of Asa's doctors! We are not talking about quacks, but problems with *bona fide* doctors. Too often we think doctors are "all-wise saviors" whose judgments are not to be questioned.

Physician Walter Bartz well says,

The attraction of cure as the appropriate end product of medical care is evident. It is logical, simple, and final. . . . It is winning. It is the good guy in the white hat. . . . It is a quick fix, the easy way. . . . The physician as Rambo.

Nothing is more important than open communication between you and your doctor. Norman Cousins tells about receiving over three thousand letters from doctors in about a dozen countries. The letters showed general agreement that modern medication is becoming increasingly dangerous and that physicians should counsel patients not to rely on drugs.

At times doctors become defensive when we question their judgment or ask for second opinions. They suffer from what Norman Cousins calls "the hardening of the categories." While we have no right to "play doctor" and make claims to being medical specialists, we *do* know our own bodies, and we have a longer, more intimate history of ourselves than doctors do. As Albert Schweitzer reminded us, there is a doctor within us!

Poor old Asa. He must have suffered terribly in those days before the advent of modern medicine. I sometimes wonder if his doctors proved more a liability than an asset. Whenever doctors stifle our questions, however stupid, or refuse to talk openly with us, Asa's doctors reappear in modern dress.

GREAT PHYSICIAN,
We know you heal through doctors
and sometimes without them.
We pray that whenever doctors cannot do good,
they may be kept from doing harm.
AMEN.

61

Hospitals:Towers of Babble
or Temples of Grace?
READ GENESIS 11:1-9 AND HEBREWS 13:1-3

Remember always to welcome strangers, for by doing this,
some people have entertained angels without knowing it.
(Hebrews 13:2, NJB)

AS A HOSPITAL CHAPLAIN, I SOMETIMES have to read patient charts, and their strange codes never cease to amaze me. For instance, what do the following abbreviations mean to patients: a.c., b.i.d., C.C., EEG, Fx, Hb, I&O, MI, n.p.o., Px, q.i.d., RUQ, Sig, TAT, or WC? I used to think that the letters n.p.o. on a patent's door meant "not permitted outside," instead of their rightful meaning, "nothing by mouth" (*non per os*).

I learned more medical babble when I had my surgery. I had a diagnosis of BPH, although my PSA was not elevated. I had the choice of a TURP or TULIP for surgery, and my surgeon expressed the hope that I would not suffer a UTI when it was over!

Charles B. Inlander and Ed Weiner express a fascinating thought:

Legend has it that the Tower of Babel was a hospital. And as soon as all of the people scurrying about on the upper tower began speaking a language that no one else could understand, they were sent down to speak to the patients.

Hospital personnel *do* speak in a strange tongue. While it may be perfectly acceptable to them to speak in such a way, it sometimes does the patient a disservice. Patients need to understand information about their condition and their care.

I am reminded of the vivid contrast between the Tower of Babel and what happened on the day of Pentecost. The builders of the tower who sought to elevate their power by "making a name for themselves" ended in confusion of language with no understanding of one another's speech. On the Day of Pentecost they were "all together in one place," and experienced such a miracle of communication that "in our own languages we hear them speaking about God's deeds of power" (Acts 2:11, NRSV).

Beyond the language and culture of the times, people were moved in their hearts and discovered a new language.

Hospitals should be places of grace where strangers are welcomed and procedures are explained in *simple* language. By not communicating with us in our own language, medical personnel are hindering our healing.

LORD,
When we remember how simply Jesus spoke,
we are ashamed that our speech is so complicated.
Help us to be direct and honest with doctors and nurses,
and expect the same from them.
AMEN.

62

Deborah, Rebekah's Nurse
READ GENESIS 35:1-8

But we were gentle among you,
like a nurse tenderly caring for her own children.
(1 Thessalonians 2:7b, NRSV)

I DOUBT THAT MANY PEOPLE KNOW THAT a nurse is named in the Bible. Her name was Deborah, and she is mentioned in passing in the Book of Genesis. She was apparently highly valued by Jacob. He must have loved her dearly, as witnessed by the deep grief he expressed at her death. She was buried under an oak tree near Bethel, which was named "Oak of Weeping" (Gen. 35:8). It would be difficult to measure the influence Deborah had on Jacob. She had been nurse to his mother, Rebekah, and she may well have been Jacob's primary caregiver during his childhood.

Little is known about how Deborah nursed Jacob. Did she spend most of her time with him, while Rebekah ran her household? Was it Deborah who took time to tell Jacob the stories of his grandfather, Abraham? Did she nurse Jacob through childhood diseases? We do not know. But we do know Jacob loved her dearly, grieved her loss, and must have returned to her grave to hallow her memory.

No one who has been sick will minimize the importance of nurses. Though the doctor has primary responsibility for the patient's care, it is the nurse who has the awesome task of helping the patient with her or his needs. Frequently "the buck stops with the nurse," for it is he or she who is mainly accountable for patient care.

Nurses run the risk of becoming too emotionally involved with their patients. Fearful of such overinvolvement, and perhaps scarred by it, some nurses adopt a cold detachment toward their patients. That is understandable, but nurses are primary caregivers, the ones who usually "hear" how a person feels when they are sick. Paul told the Thessalonians that he cared for them like a nurse, and there is little doubt that nurses are the ones who give that tender, loving care when people are sick.

I recall one occasion when I was going into surgery, and the nurse anesthetist was a former student of mine. I mumbled to her, "You were one of my students. How did you do in my course?"

She replied, "I did well."

"Good," I said. "If I didn't fail you then, don't fail me now!" Nurses have never failed me in being the persons who showed care.

Take a moment now, whether you are in the hospital or at home, or a caregiver, to remember nurses who have ministered to you. Say a prayer of gratitude for them, and ask God to be with them as they go about their work.

PRAY THE DAILY PRAYER OF MOTHER TERESA:
Dearest Lord, may I see you today
and every day in the person of your sick,
and whilst nursing them, minister unto you.
AMEN.

63

From the Other Side of the Bed
READ ISAIAH 53:1-6

Jesus said to them, "Surely you will quote this proverb to me:
'Physician heal yourself!'"
(Luke 4:23, NIV)

EVERYONE SHOULD SEE THE MOVIE *The Doctor*, in which William Hurt plays an extraordinary surgeon who becomes an ordinary patient and begins to see things a little differently when he is on the other side of the bed. His whole attitude toward sickness changes when he has to experience some of the comic errors and tragedies of being a hospital patient. At the end of the movie, he demands that every medical student be admitted as a "patient" to experience what it is like when the shoe is on the other foot.

Bernie Siegel, whose books on healing have helped me think in new ways about health and illness, underscores this need when he says,

> I would insist that doctors experience what it is like to be ill themselves. I'd like to see each doctor put into a hospital where he or she is not known, with a diagnosis of a life-threatening illness. He or she would stay there for a week and see how such patients are treated.

When Jesus visited his home town synagogue at Nazareth, he spoke from the suffering servant passage of Second Isaiah. Then he said that they would surely quote the proverb to him, "Physician, heal yourself." What they did not know was that this Jesus of Nazareth *was* a whole person. He could heal others because his life was filled with God's Spirit. Matthew tells us that Jesus healed all the sick (Matt. 8:16). Then he declares that Jesus fulfilled the prophecy of the servant from Second Isaiah: "He took up our infirmities and carried our diseases" (Matt. 8:17, NIV).

This person who never had to know sickness or disease was carrier of our diseases. This Second Adam who alone could be spared the sorrows of sickness and the sting of death bore ours. So Peter declares, "By his wounds you have been healed" (1 Pet. 2:24, NIV).

Siegel hopes that one day doctors will be treated like the "natives" so that they will be able to say to patients, "I have some understanding of what you're going through. I have experienced this, too." We all know that caregivers are far more compassionate and understanding with those who are sick when they have been through it themselves.

A gap remains between the sickbed and those who are well, between the comforted and the comforters. But we have a great Physician, Jesus Christ, who allowed his life to stand in that gap, bear the pain, and experience the anguish. So we can always turn to Jesus as one who does understand.

GOD WITH US,
In Christ you have proved how much you care.
In his suffering for and with us,
he has identified with all who are sick.
What happens to us, happens to him.
Let us take comfort in that.
AMEN.

64

Bringing Soul into the Hospital
READ LUKE 10:25-37

But a Samaritan . . . came where the man was;
and when he saw him, he took pity on him.
He went to him and bandaged his wounds.
(Luke 10:33-34, NIV)

THOMAS MOORE, IN HIS EXTRAORDINARY BOOK about the life of the spirit, talks about introducing "soul" into hospitals. He says,

> Our hospitals are generally not equipped to deal with the soul in illness. But it wouldn't take much to change them, because the soul doesn't require expensive technology and highly trained experts.

The word *hospital* comes from *hospes*, which means both "stranger" and "host." Hospitals should be places where strangers can find rest and care.

Since it is related to the word "hospitality," hospitals should be hospitable places. Henri Nouwen describes such "hospitality" in words that could be applied to hospitals:

> We can offer a space where people are encouraged to disarm themselves, to lay aside their occupations and preoccupations and to listen with attention and care to the voices speaking in their own center.

The Samaritan in Jesus' parable is forever a model for hospital care. Not only did he "see" the man who was hurt (while others passed by), he got involved with him at personal risk and bandaged his wounds. Furthermore, his care did not end with this "emergency room care," but he made sure that others would care after he left. His motive was compassion for a hurt person whose name he did not know. That was *real* hospitality. That is what hospitals need to be.

Among other things, Thomas Moore suggests that "soul" can be brought into hospitals by having "the patients be encouraged to keep track of their impressions and their emotions during their time in the hospital and . . . to note their dreams every day." He also advocates an art room and "a time and place where patients could tell stories about their illnesses and hospitalization."

John Katonah declares that hospitalization brings varying experiences for people. "For some it is a time of personal transformation and growth, for others it is a stultifying period marked by rhetorical questioning and bitter resentment." I have known both feelings. But what really matters is that "[hospitalization] can . . . be a time of sacred journeying—leaving us, upon discharge, prepared to embrace life anew, with new skills and strengths that we have come to discover." Such will be the day when "soul" is brought into hospitals.

GOD WHO IS EVERYWHERE,
*Be with us in the hospital, and here
may we not only gain health,
but find our souls.*
AMEN.

65

Left with a Limp
READ GENESIS 32:22-32

The sun rose upon him as he passed Penuel,
limping because of his hip.
(Genesis 32:31, NRSV)

JACOB EMERGED FROM THAT STRANGE, midnight struggle at Penuel with a decided limp that remained with him the rest of his life. He seemed to be winning the long battle, but the stranger touched the hollow of his thigh, and he was helpless. It was almost as if this stranger had held back until the very last, so Jacob would acknowledge that his defeat was final.

One has to admire the tenacity of Jacob. Others might have given up, whining, "It just isn't worth it! I can't stand it anymore." But this man of God's own choosing cried, "I will not let you go unless you bless me" (Gen. 32:26).

What Jacob discovered in the darkness that became a new dawn was that this stranger, God, would not let *him* go. God blessed him and gave him a new name, symbolic of new beginnings. So he limped into the future, crippled, yet crowned; broken, yet together. The old "wheeler dealer" had become the new "wounded healer."

Jacob's halting limp was his reminder that his strength came from God, not from his own clever schemes. We also face our midnight conflicts, and our struggles often focus on sickness. Sometimes physical problems won't go away. At other times recurrent memories are equally painful. Yet our limping lifestyle can become an instance of spiritual greatness.

Jacob was given a new name, Israel, for he became a new person, stronger in his weakness. So we limp into the future, scathed, but triumphant. We have learned (in those nights that never seemed to end) who held us in the darkest moments—a God who holds us with everlasting love.

Many times when leaving a hospital room tense with scared people, I have quietly said these words, "Remember this: 'The eternal God *is* your refuge, and underneath are the everlasting arms'" (Deut. 33:27, NIV). We all need to know whose we are.

George Matheson became blind, and his fiancée abandoned him. But he penned the words about a "love that would not let us go."

> O love that wilt not let me go,
> I rest my weary soul in Thee;
> I give Thee back the life I owe,
> That in Thine ocean depths its flow
> May richer, fuller be.

TENACIOUS GOD,
We do not need to be told that you are the God
who never lets us get away with our sins.
We know that too well.
What we need to hear is that you are the God
whose love never lets us go.
Today we will find peace in that.
AMEN.

66

Wounded Becomes Whole
REREAD GENESIS 32:22-32

Then the man said, "Your name will no longer be Jacob, but Israel. . . ." [Israel *means* he struggles with God.]
(Genesis 32:28a, NIV)

TWO OF THE MOST INSIGHTFUL BOOKS ON spiritual issues of sickness are Max Lerner's *Wrestling with an Angel*, and Arthur W. Frank's *At the Will of the Body*. Both books make the Penuel experience of Jacob a paradigm of sickness and health.

Lerner says, "It is the theme of this memoir that all illness and healing, all aging, all living and dying, are a wrestling with the angel. We get wounded and are preserved—or not."

Frank recognizes some of his situation in that midnight struggle where Jacob wrestles with an angel. He makes this story his own personal mythology of illness. As Jacob holds on with a grip not of violence but of need, and is blessed as a gift of God, so illness can bring blessing.

Frank says,

Wounded, Jacob becomes whole. Whole, he is renamed. . . . This is what it is to be ill: to wrestle through the long night, injured, and if you prevail until the sun rises, to receive a blessing.

I know an incredible story that parallels Jacob's wrestling with the angel. My friend Fred had undergone surgery for a massive brain tumor. He survived the surgery, but was left with slurred speech, partly damaged vision, and other disabilities which prevented him from returning to his job. Yet, his courage and contagious humor have been a witness to everyone. "I have learned two lessons from this experience," he said. "Pain is inevitable, but misery is optional, and I chose not to despair; God can use any ordeal as a blessing."

Fred is still struggling to find some viable work he can do at home. His long-term disability insurance is reviewing his case and may rule in their favor. Being disabled by surgery and unable to find some employment would be obstacles many people would find too hard to surmount. Yet Fred continues to believe and pray. He even asked my prayers for wisdom to choose the right path. He is wounded, but whole.

I remember how he brought tears to my eyes when I visited him a few weeks after his surgery. He looked at me through pained eyes and said, "I still thank God that he chose me to bear this cross. I know God will give me strength to see it through." Wounded, but whole.

LIVING CHRIST,
Our hearts recall how you came out of the tomb
and into the light of the resurrection morning,
showed your disciples your wounds.
Thank you for giving us hope that even when we are hurt,
we are healed.
AMEN.

67

Return to the Land of the Living
READ PSALM 27

I am still confident of this:
I will see the goodness of the LORD in the land of the living.
(Psalm 27:13, NIV)

IT WAS MY FIRST SUNDAY BACK AT CHURCH. As we left the sanctuary, the minister said, "Welcome back to the land of the living." I am not sure he realized his words were scriptural! The writer of Psalm 27 had experienced some serious illness and expressed his feelings in what G. Campbell Morgan called "The Psalm of a Convalescent."

Despite his problems, the psalmist ends with a confident word, "I will see the goodness of the Lord in the land of the living." Serious illness is a small death in life. For a time we exist in a shadowy world of unknown realities, prolonged inactivity, and some significant changes in lifestyle. We *do* return to the land of the living when we get better.

No writer has helped me more in understanding what recovery from sickness means than Arthur W. Frank. For him, recovery was like "being spit back into life by the great fish of illness."

Frank believes that there should be "rituals of recovery" when persons get better. Such rituals would symbolize a rebirth, that life has begun again. After all, we have "welcome home" parties for people who have been in the military or worked overseas. Rituals of recovery could become part of the church's liturgy for those who have been restored to health.

Frank also says that recovery has some inherent dangers.

> When I feel I have no time to walk out and watch the sunlight on the river, my recovery has gone too far.... When I was ill, all I wanted was to get back into the ordinary flux of activity. Now that I am back in the ordinary, I have to retain a sense of wonder at being here.

I am blessed to have health restored, with some restrictions in lifestyle. But I am all the more confident of the "goodness of the Lord in the land of the living."

PRAYER OF BONHOEFFER
O heavenly Father,
I praise and thank you
For the peace of this night;
I praise and thank you for this new day;
I praise and thank you for all your goodness
and faithfulness throughout my life.

You have granted me many blessings;
Now let me also accept what is hard
from your hand.
You will lay on me no more
than I can bear.
You make all things work together for good
for your children.
AMEN.

VII

What Sickness Teaches

Suffering finds all of us, someday.

It is then that we feel alone, isolated.

It may be only then that we are driven deep inside ourselves,

the thing we never had time for before.

By faith we may find the suffering Christ,

suffering not for himself,

but for us.

INSCRIPTION ON A WALL AT ST. JOSEPH'S HOSPITAL,

ASHEVILLE, NORTH CAROLINA

68

Laughter Is Good Medicine
READ JOHN 15:1-11

*A cheerful heart is good medicine,
but a crushed spirit dries up the bones.
(Proverbs 17:22, NIV)*

IN RECENT YEARS THE MEDICAL PROFESSIONS have been getting serious about the place of humor in the healing process. Dr. Raymond A. Moody, Jr., a practicing physician, has written a book entitled *Laugh after Laugh* in which he discusses the powerful effect of laughter on the healing process.

At DeKalb General Hospital in Decatur, Georgia, patients who seemed close to giving up were given an unusual prescription. They spent a few hours in the "humor room," viewing videotapes of old films of Laurel and Hardy and W.C. Fields, and reruns of other comedy films. After spending a few days in the humor room, many patients discovered the will to get well.

The writer of the Proverbs knew the powerful effect that laughter has on health. "A cheerful heart is good medicine. . . ." A cheerful outlook on life and laughter *are* good medicine. A cheerful heart cannot be produced by a drug company and encased in a capsule.

Ralph Waldo Emerson well said that "mirth is the medicine of God." Martin Luther said that he didn't want to go to heaven if God didn't enjoy a good joke!

Jesus was a person who loved to laugh. Touches of humor can be found in many of his parables and sayings. I am sure he must have laughed heartily with his disciples and friends. His healing laughter helped people realize that, like a ray of sunshine piercing a dark and overcast sky, laughter brings us into the presence of God.

The bottom line for Christians is that life is not only grimness, but grace. This is not to bypass the pain or discomfort that comes with sickness. There are some things in life which are *not* laughing matters. Nothing hurts more than someone dismissing our pain with flippant humor. Reinhold Niebuhr said it well, "Humor must move toward faith or sink into despair when ultimate issues are raised." Most of life, however, can be redeemed by a saving sense of humor.

On the night before facing the brutal horror of the cross, Jesus said to the disciples, "I have told you this that my joy might be in you and that your joy may be complete" (John 15:11, NIV). Jesus knew that joy can be found in the presence of pain. As the writer of the Hebrews says, "Let us fix our eyes on Jesus, the author and perfecter of our faith, who for the joy set before him endured the cross" (Heb. 12:2, NIV).

Laughter *is* good medicine. It is great for the circulation, releases tension and prolongs life. Will Rogers summed it up well when he said, "We are here just for a spell—so get a few laughs."

JOYFUL GOD,
Help us to get a few laughs today.
AMEN.

69

Accepted Limitations
READ ACTS 16:6-10

*When they came to the border of Mysia,
they tried to enter Bithynia,
but the Spirit of Jesus would not allow them to.
(Acts 16:7,NIV)*

ROBERT W. MCCLELLAND TELLS A STORY ABOUT a book-lover who was talking to a man who couldn't care less about old books. In cleaning out his attic he had just thrown one away. "Why did you do that?" asked the collector. "Oh, it was old and beat up, printed by a man named Guten-something." Said the other, "You are mad! That was a Gutenberg Bible, worth about $400,000." "Naw," said the man, unmoved. "It wouldn't have brought anything anyway. Some fellow named Luther had written all over the margins." How often it is true that when people show wear and tear or experience limitations in life, we devalue them.

Paul wanted to take the gospel to Bithynia, and no wonder, for Bithynia was one of the richest provinces of Asia Minor. It would have been a crowning success to bring Christianity there. But the way was blocked, and he landed in Troas. Paul's dreams were denied, his plans thwarted, and his hopes limited. Yet he found God's purpose still at work in Macedonia.

Peace comes when we accept our limits. Sickness brings its limitations, especially in older age. Donald X. Burt tells about the changes it brings.

My days of wine and roses are over; now I am in my nights of Maalox and frequent risings. . . . My mind is awake and functioning at "dawn's early light," but all that is below is problematic.

Augustine, who was plagued by illness of one kind or another for most of his seventy-six years, still praised the body as the temple of the Spirit. He wrote,

Other animals are bent over towards the ground but we humans are made to walk upright looking at the heavens. . . . It makes you wonder at how great the soul must be considering how finely molded is its container, the body.

I have learned the joy of quieter days and the freedom that comes from realizing that if people are to love me now, it is *not* for what I can *do* for them, but what I can *be* with them.

I often think of the prayer of St. Francis de Sales:

Do not fear what may happen tomorrow. The same loving Father who cares for you today will care for you tomorrow and every day. Either he will shield you from suffering or he will give you unfailing strength to bear it. Be at peace, then, and put aside all anxious thoughts and imaginings.

EVER-PRESENT HELP,
*Whatever our limitations, however many times
our plans are thwarted and our efforts denied,
we can be at peace if we know you give us unfailing strength.*
AMEN.

70

Men Can Be Weak, Too
READ 1 CORINTHIANS 2:1-5

*And I came to you in weakness
and in fear and in much trembling.*
(1 Corinthians 2:3, NRSV)

IN YEARS GONE BY MEN WITH ILLNESS were expected to remain strong and silent and keep their feelings under lock and key. "Be a real man! Only wimps cry. Bite your lip and be brave," we were told. Men were also programmed to view their bodies as machines, which needed only a repair job to solve the problem.

Thank God that view *is* changing. But vestiges of the old machismo remain. I discovered that when I went through prostate surgery and experienced the "gland illusion" that I could discuss my problem with other men. I discovered that a polite silence still surrounds discussion of "male" problems, especially since they often denote weakness and advanced age.

Now I realize that one would not expect to hear prostate problems discussed by the "good old boys" at the Testosterone Cafe, but I seriously question why this prevalent problem that affects ninety percent of men past fifty years of age has to remain such a well-kept secret.

I found myself being more assertive with men about openly discussing this problem and discovered that many men wanted to talk about it. It is all right to be human. Paul Tournier has said,

Yes, sometimes the strength which comes from God—his grace—heals; sometimes it lifts us out of our weakness; but sometimes, too, it leaves our weakness with us, and gives us a quite different strength—the strength to accept it.

The apostle Paul, commenting on his visit to the city of Corinth, surely used no typical "macho" terms to describe his presence. Rather, he came "in weakness and fear and in much trembling." He surely was not ashamed to tell about his weaknesses (see 2 Cor. 11:16-30).

I admit that I still have residual feelings about revealing weakness, admitting my vulnerability. In several episodes of excruciating pain during some post-op procedures in the hospital, I wanted to "be brave." Thank God one of the nurses told me, "Go ahead and scream. We understand!"

Sam Keen underscores the need for men to express their feelings when he says in *Fire in the Belly,*

Since boys are taught not to cry, men must learn to weep. After a man passes through arid numbness, he comes to a tangled jungle of grief and unnamed sorrow. The path to a manly heart runs through the valley of tears.

LOVING CHRIST,
In you there is neither male nor female.
Help us to realize our common need to be weak,
for our weakness can become your strength.
AMEN.

67

67

67

71

Turtle Pace, No Wild Goose Chase
READ DEUTERONOMY 8:1-5

*Better is a handful with quiet than two handfuls with toil,
and a chasing after wind.*
(Ecclesiastes 4:6, NRSV)

MOSES LOOKED BACK AT THE WILDERNESS experience as a high moment in Israel's journey of faith. He reminded the Israelites, "Remember the long way the LORD your God has led you these forty years in the wilderness . . ." (Deut. 8:3, NRSV). At first they grumbled and complained about the delay. They wanted to go right into the land of promise, but they had to be disciplined in the desert. God knew that without this wilderness they would never have had the stability or strength to survive their enemies, or the enemy within them.

God slowed them down to a turtle pace. But at least they did not go on a wild goose chase, never to realize their destiny. It is the same with the delays that sickness causes us. We get fretful and anxious when it takes time to recover from sickness. We hate delays. We want to be busy. Why? We cling to the view that what we *do* gives us worth. So, afraid we do not have enough worth, we push ourselves harder and harder, taking on additional projects in our pursuit of acceptance. But recovering from surgery or a long sickness forces us to slow down. And we resist, at times, the slower pace. We want to be busy.

Thomas Merton believed that when we give in to busyness, we are practicing a subtle form of violence.

There is a pervasive form of contemporary violence... [and that is] activism and overwork. The rush and pressure of modern life are a form, perhaps the most common form, of its innate violence.

To allow oneself to be carried away by a multitude of conflicting concerns, to surrender to too many demands, to commit oneself to too many projects, to want to help everyone in everything, is to succumb to violence.

Yes, it is true that encounters with sickness slow us down, and even when we return to the "normal routine" we discover some of our old resiliency has gone. But there is blessing in this. We learn that frantic busyness renders us deaf to what is healing, both in ourselves and in others. The word *absurd* comes from the Latin word, *surdus*, which means "deaf."

The writer of Ecclesiastes cites a proverb, "Better is a handful with quiet than two handfuls with toil, and a chasing after wind." Sickness does slow us down, and we become restless about our slowed-down pace. I have learned that this quiet time can be prime time for hearing what God is saying to us.

GOD OF INNER PEACE,
When we become fretful and frantic about
how much we can't do,
or how our sickness has made us slow down,
remind us of the value of quiet.
AMEN.

72

Patience NOW
READ PSALM 40

In your patience possess ye your souls.
(Luke 21:19, KJV)

ONE OF MY BESETTING SINS IS IMPATIENCE. I became so preoccupied with my timetable for getting better that I fretted over the long weeks of delay. Four weeks after surgery I expressed my impatience in a journal entry.

The days seem so *empty,* especially for one whose days had been so full. Even reading books is getting "old," and I reached the edges of despair with these long days of discomfort.

Psalm 40 reflects a person who learned patience. "I waited patiently for the Lord . . . " he begins, and ends with these words, "You are my help and deliverer; do not delay, O my God" (Psalm 40:17, NRSV). For him, patience was not stoic acceptance of things as they were, but taking a risk of faith that God would deliver.

The long wait for healing purges the soul. Richard Foster says, "So often we hide our true condition with the surface virtues of pious activity, but, once the leaves of our frantic pace drop away, the transforming power of a wintry spirituality can have effect." Sickness *is* a winter of the soul, but also opportunity for spiritual rebirth if we possess our souls in patience.

William F. May says, "Patience requires purposive waiting, receiving, willing; it demands a more intense sort of activity; it requires taking control of one's spirit precisely when all else goes out of control, when panic would send us sprawling in all directions." That kind of patience means that even when panic becomes a possibility, we maintain control and wait for healing.

Harry Emerson Fosdick told a story of a curious practice of apple growers in Maine. A friend visiting the orchard one day saw the trees so laden with apples that branches had to be propped up to keep them off the ground. When he questioned the owner about it, the owner said, "Go look at the tree's trunk near the bottom." The visitor saw that the tree had been badly wounded with a deep gash. "That is something we have learned about trees," the owner said. "When the tree tends to wood and leaves, and not to fruit, we gash it, and almost always—no one knows why—this is the result. It turns energies into fruit."

The gashes of delay, discomfort, and pain teach patience, one of the fruits of the Spirit. So "we . . . rejoice in our sufferings, because we know that suffering produces perseverance; perseverance, character; and character, hope (Rom. 5:3-4, NIV). Be patient with sickness and it *will* bear the fruit of character.

LORD,
Teach me the art of patience whilst I am well,
and give me the use of it when I am sick.
In that day either lighten my burden or strengthen my back.
Make me, who so often in my health have discovered my
weakness presuming on my own strength,
to be strong in my sickness when I solely rely on thy
assistance.
AMEN.
(Prayer of Thomas Fuller)

73

Mourning Our Losses
READ PHILIPPIANS 3:7-11

But whatever was to my profit
I now consider loss for the sake of Christ.
What is more, I consider everything a loss compared to the
surpassing greatness of knowing Christ Jesus my Lord.
(Philippians 3:7-8, NIV)

ONE OF THE LESSONS SICKNESS TAUGHT ME was the importance of mourning my losses. I learned that my problems with mourning were not caused by the losses, but by other people's demands that I get my mourning over with. When we mourn our losses it reminds others of their mortality. People pressure us to return to the healthy mainstream and forget our losses.

But it is important to mourn our losses. Jesus called blessed the person who mourns (Matt. 5:4). What I mourned the most was loss of vigor and energy. Although I improved after surgery, I am not quite the same as I was before. That can be especially true if you are older and face the inevitable decline of the years. Things just don't work as well as they once did. Sometimes the body doesn't carry out what the mind commands. R. Scott Sullender says,

One of the inevitable losses that everyone faces in later life is the gradual loss of health. All of us will experience this loss unless we die unexpectedly at an early age. . . . The loss of health is experienced as a gradual decline, peppered with many points of realization when we are keenly aware of what we have lost.

This gradual loss of health can be accentuated if our body is altered by surgery. We spend a lifetime building our images of our physical selves, only to have them shattered by loss. We can no longer believe the old aphorism, "Tomorrow you will be as good as ever."

But we can transcend preoccupation with our bodies. We can rise above our losses. Paul certainly did. He tells the Philippian Christians that what he formerly considered "gain" was now loss for the sake of Christ. In fact, "everything (was) a loss compared to the surpassing greatness of knowing Christ."

Visiting the terminally ill in hospitals unearths some vivid contrasts in attitudes. Some surrender to anger and bitterness and become spiritual invalids. Others take the spiritual option of functioning the best they can, finishing the course; they touch others by their valiant struggle.

We *do* need to mourn our losses. They are real and touch us deeply. But we are also called by God to learn to rise above our losses, focus our life on the things of the spirit, and stay focused there even as "our nature is wasting away." "This is the victory that conquers the world, our faith."

UNDERSTANDING FATHER,
You want us to grieve our losses,
not rush into life without gaining the perspective of pain.
Help us to mourn
and then move on to a greater faith.
AMEN.

74

A Spirituality for Sickness
READ PSALM 6

Beloved, I pray that all may go well with you
and that you may be in good health,
just as it is well with your soul.
(3 John 2, NRSV)

SOMETIME DURING MY RECOVERY AT HOME I received an interesting get-well card that quoted a verse from Third John, a little known New Testament book. The author prayed that the readers might be in good health, and added, "just as it is well with your soul."

Nothing is more vital than good health. Nothing tears at our spirit more than sickness. We *do* want to be cured, but there is a spiritual healing that transcends cure. Many people discover that healing is delayed, or comes only in part, or never comes fully to our bodies. Even when a final cure is not possible, we can be spiritually healthy.

Sickness does make us vulnerable to spiritual growth. Nothing is more symbolic of the vulnerability of sick persons than the old-style hospital gown, with its open back and string ties, revealing as much as it conceals. We devote much of life to covering up our identities. Hospitalization, symbolized by the hospital gown, invites us to be vulnerable and open to a spiritual journey.

The author of Psalm 6 pleads with God to end his sickness. "O LORD, heal me, for my bones are shaking with terror" (Psalm 6:2, NRSV). He pleads for deliverance from sickness and death by appealing to God's steadfast love. God hears his prayer (v. 9), and he is vindicated and finds peace. It *is* well with his soul.

Horatio G. Spafford was the father of five children, an active member of a Presbyterian church in Chicago, and a loyal supporter of D.L. Moody and other evangelical leaders of the nineteenth century. Suddenly his life tumbled in. His only son unexpectedly died. The great Chicago fire of 1871 wiped out his extensive real estate investments. He decided to take his family to Europe to join the Moody crusades there but was detained by urgent business. He sent his wife and four daughters on the S.S. *Ville du Harve,* planning to join them later.

Halfway across the Atlantic, the ship was struck by an English vessel and sank in twelve minutes. All four of his daughters drowned. Mrs. Spafford was among the few who were miraculously saved. Spafford stood for hours at a time on the deck of the ship carrying him to rejoin his sorrowing wife in Cardiff, Wales. When the ship passed the approximate place where the girls had drowned, Spafford wrote the words of the hymn, "It Is Well with My Soul."

When peace, like a river, attendeth my way,
When sorrows like sea billows roll;
Whatever my lot, thou hast taught me to say,
It is well, it is well with my soul.

GRACIOUS GOD,
Help us today to truthfully say,
"It is well with my soul,"
no matter what our circumstances may be.
Then we will find health.
AMEN.

75

Coming Out of a Tomb
READ JOHN 11:17-44

I will not die but live,
and will proclaim what the Lord has done.
(Psalm 118:17, NIV)

ANYONE WHO FACES SICKNESS CONFRONTS death. When you go under anesthesia you wonder if you will wake up. Facing the uncertainty of test results which may indicate cancer leaves you face-to-face with death. Despite society's recurring efforts to deny death, sickness makes you realize its inevitability. As Lucretius observed in his memorable poem, "Suppose you could contrive to live for centuries. As many as you will. Death, even so, will still be waiting for you."

I've often wondered what Lazarus must have told his sisters about his experience of dying and coming back. Did it affect his relationships? What about his use of time? What kinds of things changed after being called from the tomb?

Henri Nouwen, whose near-death experience is related in his book *Beyond the Mirror,* tells about learning what it meant not to have died.

> I was glad to be alive, but on a deeper level I was confused and wondered why it was that Jesus had not yet called me home. . . . I also knew that living longer on this earth would mean more struggle, more pain, more anguish, and more loneliness.

Nouwen's "post-mortem" life made each day more precious. But he knew that his experience of God's love in his moment of crisis could easily disappear when "the addictive powers of everyday existence make their presence felt again."

I know the feeling. My own "deliverance" from serious complications after surgery left me grateful to God for some extra years. I, too, have learned the meaning of what Paul Tillich called "the eternal now." But there remains that sinking feeling that the spiritual insights received *will* fade away as life returns to some semblance of normalcy.

Nouwen beautifully describes the meaning of the accident which brought him to the portals of death. Commenting on his friends' congratulations on his recovery, and mindful of his own question, "Would it not have been preferable to have been completely set free from this ambiguous world?" Nouwen finds his answer. "I wonder more and more whether I am not given some extra years so that I can live them from the other side." Such is our mission when we recover from sickness.

GOD OF NEW LIFE,
As we come out of the tomb of sickness,
may we continue to see life with the new
sight we have gained from "the other side."
AMEN.

76

Healing Is Up to Us!
READ DEUTERONOMY 30:15-20

*I have set before you life and death,
blessing and cursing; therefore choose life.
(Deuteronomy 30:19, NKJV)*

SICKNESS BRINGS MANY CHOICES; choice of a doctor, a hospital, second opinions when surgery is suggested. Max Lerner says that "everyone stricken with some 'dread' disease must at some point confront the question of how much to talk about, and how much to reveal."

Norman Cousins accentuates the power of our choice. Denying that "the center of the healing process is lodged with the physician," he says, "It is lodged within the individual, and the wise physician knows how to summon and release it."

The Deuteronomist makes sure the Israelites realize they have the choice of life or death, blessings or cursings. And he might have added, health or sickness. We can be bitter, or get better; we can be healed or hung up by our illness.

Wayne Muller relates the story of a young rabbi who wanted to be recognized for his wisdom, but the people of the village never gave him the honor he expected. When an old rabbi famous for his wisdom came to the village, the clever young rabbi saw this as a great opportunity to show his superiority. He planned to approach the older rabbi holding a tiny bird in his hand. He would ask him the following question, "Rabbi, is this bird dead or alive?" If the rabbi answered, "The bird is alive," the young man could easily crush the small creature and hold it out for all to see. If the old rabbi said the bird was dead, he would simply let the bird fly away into the sky.

The next day, when the old rabbi sat before the assembled villagers, the young man stood up and said, "Rabbi, since you are all wise, tell me if this bird I hold behind my back is dead or alive." The old rabbi was silent for a moment, and then looked at the young man and said, "It's up to you, my friend, it's up to you."

The person who experiences illness has problems to solve, but the deeper questions regard who we are and what attitude we will take toward our sickness. William F. May believes that "health crises . . . confront their victims with things to do; but, far more profoundly, as such crises assault identity, they force their victims to decide who and how they will be."

May Sarton writes in *Journal of a Solitude* some powerful words about what suffering can mean:

It is only when we can believe that we are creating the soul that life has any meaning, but when we can believe it—and I do and always have—then there is nothing we do that is without meaning and nothing that we suffer that does not hold the seed of creation in it.

Choose life . . . and healing!

LORD OF LIFE,
We do choose this day to use whatever has
happened to us not as a stumbling block
but as a stepping-stone to growth.
AMEN.

77

Passing It On
READ 2 CORINTHIANS 1:3-7

Blessed be the God and Father of our Lord Jesus Christ . . .
and God of all comfort, who comforts us in all our tribulation,
that we may be able to comfort those who are in any trouble,
with the comfort with which we ourselves are
comforted by God.
(2 Corinthians 1:3-4, NKJV)

PAUL MENTIONS THE NOUN *comfort* or the verb *to comfort* no fewer than nine times in these verses. From God's comfort we gain the power to comfort others who are going through hard times. Persons who have experienced sickness and all the issues that sickness brings to one's life seem to have a special sense in comforting others who face similar troubles.

How do we make ourselves available to the sick? By our prayers and our presence. Robert J. Wicks wisely says,

> We will only make sense as ministers to others when they see in our faces, hear in our words, and experience in our actions true hope, true prayerfulness. . . . With prayer we can put aside our fears and make their pain *our* pain.

The wisdom of these words is emphasized when we realize some of the occupational hazards of being comfort givers. Hospital chaplain Margot Hover says,

"One liability of our work, close as it is to illness, accident, tragedy and chaos, is that it may cause us to retreat inward, away from the harm we see so often." I can remember many times as a hospital chaplain that I left worn out and exhausted from being present to so much pain and sickness. I wanted to leave that place and never return.

I also know that some caregivers give to others because they feel unworthy to receive or because they hope to earn care in return. There are times when we become caregivers because of our own painful history. Much of my concern for frail elderly in nursing homes grows out of my mother's horrible struggle and eventual death from Parkinson's disease.

Yet God redeems that pain by calling us to comfort others, sensitized to their need by our own experience of pain and suffering. As a hospital chaplain before my surgery, I said the right words, and yet I admit there were times when I used tactics as a pastoral visitor to get out of the room when I was afraid of being engulfed by their pain.

My surgery has taught me how to be more of a caring presence to others. To suffer with another person does not mean to drown in their pain; that would be as foolish as jumping into a pool to save a drowning swimmer only to drown oneself. I may not have the cure, but I can be there as a helpful presence.

That is what the strong comfort of God does for us. We are obliged to pass it on to others.

GOD OF ALL COMFORT,
As we have received your strong comfort,
so may we comfort others.
AMEN.

78

When the Cup Doesn't Pass
READ MARK 14:32-42

*Going a little farther, he fell to the ground and prayed that
if possible the hour might pass from him.
"Abba, Father," he said, "everything is possible for you.
Take this cup from me.
Yet not what I will, but what you will."
(Mark 14:35-36, NIV)*

A FEW DAYS BEFORE SURGERY I SPENT some moments in
a small church meditating on Hofman's portrait of
Christ in Gethsemane. It was the second time that this
holy event became a focal point in my mind before
surgery. Charles de Foucauld wrote that Gethsemane is
a good place to be before any of life's trials:

So we, when we have a severe trial to undergo, or
some danger or suffering to face, go aside to pray in
solitude, and so pass the last hours that separate us
from our trial. Let us do this in every serious event in
our lives.

It seems as if Jesus experienced all of Elisabeth
Kubler-Ross's stages of death and dying in that garden.
When denial and anger are no longer present, Jesus
bargains, "Everything is possible for you. Take this cup
from me." Then, "My soul is overwhelmed with sorrow
to the point of death." Finally Jesus reaches acceptance,
"Yet not what I will, but what you will."

Although it was not God's intentional will that this cup of anguish be thrust upon him, it *was* God's will in these circumstances that Jesus should not escape the pain. Jesus' acceptance made the cross an instrument of God's redemption of the world.

What happened in Gethsemane meant much to me because I realized that if Jesus, the perfect Son of God, prayed to be spared, then my fears did not reveal a lack of faith. Sometimes the cup does not pass, the cure never comes, and we never fully recover. Yet nothing can happen to us that God cannot change for good.

In 1937 George Bernanos wrote a small, modern classic entitled *The Diary of a Country Priest*. It is the story of a young priest's struggle to overcome the powers of darkness which he found within himself and in the souls of those in his parish. At the end of the book there is a moving scene when the dying priest asks for extreme unction. Refused last rites because of his excommunication from the church, the dying priest says that grace is not restricted to the sacraments.

"Does it matter? Grace is everywhere. . . ."

Grace *is* everywhere. Grace is what Jesus experienced in the garden. Grace is what is offered to us when the cup doesn't pass.

———

GRANT, O GOD . . .
that we may never abandon the struggle,
but that we may endure to the end and so be saved,
that we may never forget that sweat is the price of all things,
and that without the cross there cannot be the crown.
AMEN.

79

Living in the Depths
READ LUKE 5:1-8

Deep calls to deep in the
roar of your waterfalls.
(Psalm 42:7, NIV)

THE DISCIPLES HAD RETURNED FROM FISHING all night in the shallow waters. Their nets were empty. Jesus stood on the shore and said to Simon, "Put out into deep water, and let down the nets for a catch." Although it seemed to be the wrong place and the wrong time, the disciples obeyed and were amazed at their catch of fish.

So much of life is lived in shallow waters. We rarely launch out into the depths to discover life's meaning. Paul Tillich has said,

> Much of our life continues on the surface. . . . We do not stop to look at the height above us, or the depth below us. . . . We are in constant motion and never stop to plunge into the depth. . . . it is only when the picture that we have of ourselves breaks down completely . . . that we are willing to look into a deeper level of our being.

Sickness forces you into the depths. So often we skate through life (often on thin ice), never exploring life's depths. Then sickness jolts us out of the shallows into the realities of life.

The story of Job ends with no answer to the question of why good people suffer, but Job's deep experience of God's presence is better than an answer. "My ears had heard of you but now my eyes have seen you" (Job 42:5). It is enough.

Tillich adds that "the name of this infinite and inexhaustible depth and ground of all being *is God*. That depth is what the word *God* means. . . . He who knows about depth knows about God." What Peter and the disciples later realized was that when they ventured into the depths and left the shallow waters, they would discover God's presence in Jesus.

Sickness brings us into the depths. It gives us opportunity to get beyond the trivialities of life and discover God's presence and power. The Hasidic Jews have a story about the sorrow tree. According to them, on Judgment Day we will be invited to hang all of our own sorrows on the tree of sorrows. When we have done that we will be given permission to walk around the tree and survey everyone else's miseries in order to select a set we like better. According to Hasidic legend, in the end we freely choose our own sorrows once more. They have brought us into the depths.

PRAY THIS PRAYER OF AUGUSTINE:
God of life,
there are days when the burdens we carry
are heavy on our shoulders and weigh us down,
when the road seems dreary and endless,
the skies gray and threatening,
when our lives have no music in them,
and our hearts are lonely,
and our souls have lost their courage.
Flood the path with light.
AMEN.

80

A Whole New Life
READ DEUTERONOMY 30:15-20

*I call heaven and earth to witness against you today that I
have set before you life and death, blessings and curses.
Choose life.*
(Deuteronomy 30:19, NRSV)

REYNOLDS PRICE WAS DIAGNOSED WITH CANCER of the
spinal chord in 1984 and defied all the odds and
medical predictions with an amazing recovery. Since
the tumor, he has completed thirteen books (he had
written twelve in the previous twenty-two years). He
writes about mystical experiences he had while battling
the cancer. One experience involved seeing Jesus
coming to him by the Sea of Galilee and saying, "Your
sins are forgiven." When he asked, "Am I also cured?"
he heard two words: "That too."

Later, while experiencing real pain from radiation
treatments, he pondered his somber prospects:
paralysis, dependence on others, untouchable pain, and
the absence of work. He recalls looking up at the ceiling
and asking God, "How much more do I take?" He
heard one word: *More.* He asked for Communion, and
felt God's presence. His answer to *More* was "Bring it
on."

What makes this story so remarkable is the whole
new life that began for Price. Reflecting on this
catastrophic illness he wrote, "If I were called on to
value honestly my present life beside my past—the

years from 1933 till '84 against the years after—I'd have to say that, despite an enjoyable fifty-year start, these recent years since full catastrophe have gone still better. They've brought more in and sent more out—more love and care, more knowledge and patience, more work in less time."

Reynolds Price recalled a "passage of daunting eloquence" in the thirtieth chapter of Deuteronomy where God gives a choice between life or death, blessings or curses. He found a frail sense of continuing purpose, the will to go on. "The illness itself either unleashed a creature within me that had been restrained, and let him run at his own hungry will; or it planted a whole new creature in place of the old." Price chose life. As he concluded, "I've yet to watch another life that seems to have brought more pleasure to its owner than mine has to me."

I stand in awe at this story. What he suffered might well have devastated me. But I *can* identify with his belief that any serious illness and recovery means a whole new life. Life is never the same. I, too, have found new energy since my close encounter—energy I never dreamed I could possess when I retired three years ago. Descent into the deep darkness of the grim pastures brings a new sense of reality . . . and a whole new self. I, too, choose life.

DEAR LORD,
You give so much, while I give so little.
I should give up everything for you,
trusting you to care for my every need. . . .
Lord, knock your grace into me that I may truly be good.
AMEN.
(Teresa of Avila)

81

From Grim to Green Pastures
READ PSALM 23

He makes me lie down in green pastures.
(Psalm 23:2a, NIV)

THERE IS ALWAYS NEW LIGHT THAT SHINES out of the Twenty-third Psalm. It is not just a word for death, but a powerful word for life. One phrase captured my attention. "He makes me lie down in green pastures." David recalled his life as a shepherd and knew that the sheep would keep eating the fresh, verdant grass of the green pastures unless they were made to lie down. So the shepherd *makes* them lie down.

Being made to "lie down" made for grim pastures for me. My active life had been taken from me and at times the discomfort and fright of my illness looked more like the "valley of the shadows." Now I realize that they were green pastures, a time for spiritual renewal and cultivation of my inner life.

Norman Cousins has shown how illness is a necessary phase of life's journey:

Illness is a natural part of life, just as birth is and as death is. It's unusual, indeed, to expect that we can get through this lifetime without some illnesses, even serious illnesses. But we haven't yet developed a philosophy of being able to deal with illness in this country.

Being forced to lie down in green pastures allows time for deepening our spiritual selves. While our bodies mend, we can pay more attention to our souls.

Sickness gradually weans a person away from roles, achievements, and preoccupations. Aspects of life once taken for granted become more appreciated. The sick person may actually experience a new sense of wonder about life.

I have experienced this wonder since my illness. With the poet Archibald MacLeish I can affirm,

> At twenty, stooping round about,
> I thought the world a miserable place,
> Truth a trick, faith in doubt,
> Little beauty, less grace.
>
> Now at sixty what I see,
> Although the world is worse by far,
> Stops my heart in ecstasy.
> God, the wonders that there are!

Being sick felt like living in grim pastures, no doubt. At times I wish I would have been spared. Now I realize that it has become a vital part of my faith journey. With the psalmist, I can face every day with that ringing affirmation,

> *Surely goodness and mercy shall follow me*
> *all the days of my life:*
> *and I will dwell in the house of the Lord for ever.*

AMEN and AMEN.

Acknowledgments

The Publisher gratefully acknowledges permission to reprint from the following copyrighted sources:

Two stanzas from "Prayers for Fellow-Prisoners, Christmas 1943, Morning Prayers" from *Letters and Papers from Prison*, revised, enlarged edition by Dietrich Bonhoeffer. Copyright © 1953, 1967, 1971 by SCM Press, Ltd. Reprinted with permission of Macmillan Publishing Company and SCM Press, Ltd.

Excerpt from *A Joseph Campbell Companion*, selected and edited by Diane Olson. Copyright © 1991 by The Joseph Campbell Foundation. Reprinted by permission of HarperCollins Publishers, Ltd.

"Prayer for a Well-Meaning Visitor" from *Patient Prayers: Talking to God from a Hospital Bed* by John V. Chervokas. Copyright © 1989 by John V. Chervokas. Reprinted by permission of The Crossroad Publishing Company.

Excerpt from "Different Pieces" by William Dugger. Used by permission of William Dugger.

Excerpts from *At the Will of the Body* by Arthur W. Frank. Copyright © 1991 by Arthur W. Frank and Catherine E. Foote. Reprinted by permission of Houghton Mifflin Company. All rights reserved.

Excerpt from "O Christ, the Healer" by Fred Pratt Green. Words copyright © 1969 by Hope Publishing Company, Carol Stream, IL 60188. All rights reserved. Used by permission.

Excerpt from "Give Us Strength" by Søren Kierkegaard from *Prayers of Kierkegaard*. Used by permission of The University of Chicago Press.

"With Age Wisdom" from *Collected Poems 1917-1982* by Archibald MacLeish. Copyright © 1985 by the Estate of Archibald MacLeish. Reprinted by permission of Houghton Mifflin Co. All rights reserved.

Excerpt from "The Telephone" by Michel Quoist from *Prayers*. Copyright © 1963 by Sheed & Ward, Inc. Kansas City, MO, USA. Used by permission of the publisher.

Excerpt from *Praying Our Goodbyes* by Joyce Rupp OSM. Copyright © 1988 by Ave Maria Press. Used by permission of the publisher.

Excerpt from *Illness as Metaphor* by Susan Sontag. Copyright © 1977, 1978 by Susan Sontag. Reprinted by permission of Farrar, Straus & Giroux, Inc. and Penguin Books, Ltd.

Excerpt from prayer in *A Private House of Prayer* by Leslie D. Weatherhead. Copyright renewal © 1986 by Lorna Caunt, A. D. Weatherhead and A. K. Weatherhead. Used by permission of Abingdon Press.

"Letter" used by permission of Alex and Jennifer White.

Excerpt from *A Return to Love* by Marianne Williamson. Copyright © 1992 by Marianne Williamson. Reprinted by permission of HarperCollins Publishers, Inc.